LALANÈ

D1495022

LASIRENELABALEINE

BOSSOU EN FEU

LALANNE
VODOO-
SOBOMASSONNIQUE

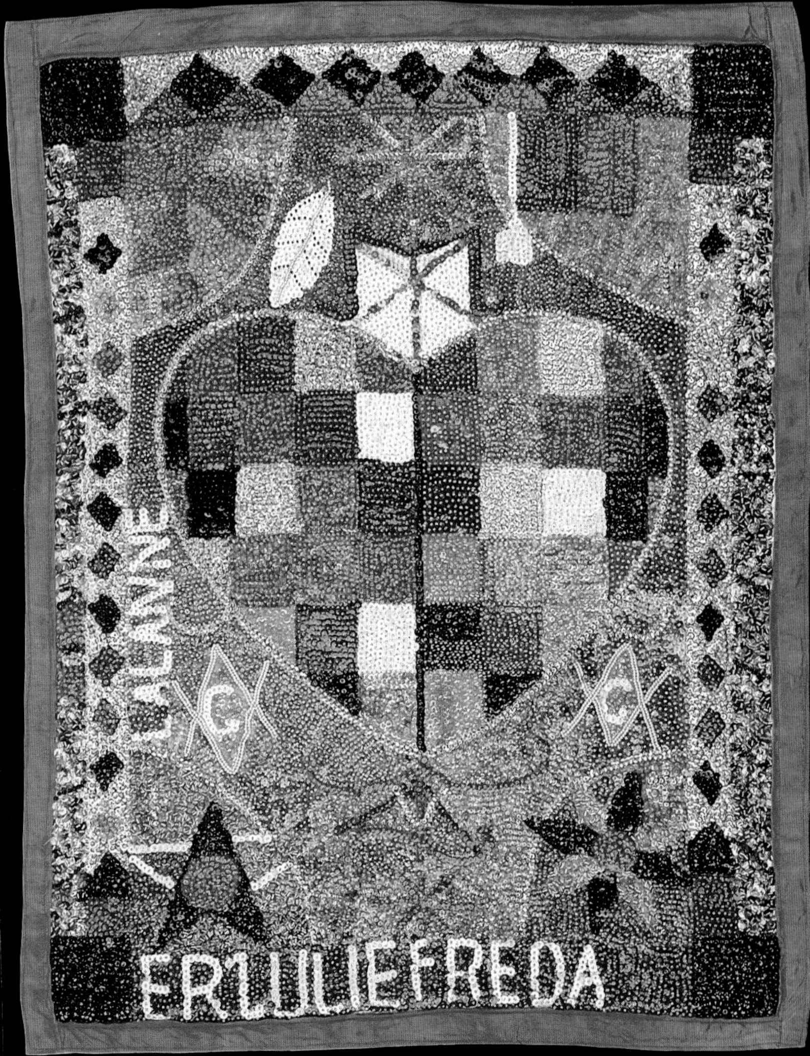
ERZULIE FREDA

CONTENTS

VOODOO
TRUTH AND FANTASY

Laënnec Hurbon

THAMES AND HUDSON

In the Fon language spoken in Benin, *vodun* means an invisible force, terrible and mysterious, which can meddle in human affairs at any time. The displacement of millions of black slaves to the New World led to the rebirth of African beliefs and practices in the Americas, under various forms and names: *candomblé* in Brazil, *santería* in Cuba, *obeayisne* in Jamaica, *shango cult* in Trinidad and *vodou* in Haiti.

CHAPTER 1
THE GREAT CROSSING

On a slave ship that has uprooted him from his native land and is taking him to the Caribbean, an African rebels (opposite). At the end of the voyage, the colonials receive the first slaves in the town of Port-de-Paix (right).

In the 17th century the African continent was little known to the Europeans, who imagined it peopled with savages steeped in idolatry and subject to the curse of Ham. However, Portugal carried on the slave trade of black Africans to the Canary Islands, where some sugar plantations had already been established. When the first Compagnie Française des Iles d'Amérique was founded in 1635, the slaves were purchased from the coastal kingdoms or acquired through raids and wars. Placed aboard ships leaving the Gulf of Guinea, they were taken first to Guadeloupe and Martinique and later to Saint-Domingue.

In the ancient kingdom of Benin

A cult dedicated to 'spirits' that rule the different realms of nature and human activities, voodoo was first encountered in Africa among the Fon, the Yoruba and the Ewe in the Gulf of Benin, in an area that stretches from Ghana to Nigeria and Togo. More specifically, it was developed in Dahomey (today the republic of Benin).

In this region, society is organized around the ethnic group, the village, the family and kinship. Each of these groups has its own *vodu* or *vodun*, ancestral and guardian deities. The cult of the dead, called *egun-gun*, brings families and tribes together in large gatherings, a festive way of ensuring that religious traditions will endure.

Ceremonies, held in convents or temples, include dancing to the beat of the drums. Animal sacrifices – cattle, sheep or chickens – are offered to the *vodun* to win their protection. The priests, *voduno* or *huno*, are responsible for guiding the faithful in their relations with the *vodun* by interpreting their messages. These

arrive in the course of ceremonies and come to rest in the body of the faithful, most frequently of the initiated, or *hounso;* the individual is said to enter into possession or become the 'horse' of a 'spirit'.

The domination of the spirits of Abomey

The relations between the different tribal groups around the Gulf of Benin are marked by tensions, animosities and frequent wars, which affect the religious life. Thus, at the beginning of the 18th century, the royal family of the city of Abomey, seeking to extend its power, decided to centralize voodoo by appropriating certain deities of its enemies, such as those of the Yoruba.

The priests, who until this point had operated independently from the political sphere, were forced to become court dignitaries. Some spirits were eliminated, while others were imposed throughout the kingdom, becoming, in effect, public *vodun.* One of these, for

Many of the 'spirits' of the Yoruba tribe of Nigeria (see mask, below) were integrated into the religion of Benin. The Temple of the Snake at Ouidah is shown here at the end of the 19th century.

example, called Agassou, is the ancestor who founded the royal line of Abomey, held by legend to be the offspring of a woman and a panther.

Fa and Legba: fate and the art of escaping it

Families and individuals nonetheless continued to honour their own *vodun.* So it is that from the 18th century one of the most important in Dahomey is Fa: originally from the kingdom of Oyo (today Nigeria), he rules over divination, revealing to the individual the *vodun* to honour as well as the proper rites to follow in order to gain its protection or appease its anger. At Ife, he is represented by a mythic palm tree from which he would have been born. Trees have a special role in ensuring the link between sky and earth and are therefore considered the dwelling places of spirits. All individuals have their own Fa, to which they are introduced in several stages: at the age of ten, at adolescence and as an adult.

Next to Fa, the personification of fate, is Legba, nicknamed the Trickster, through whose agency one may deceive fate. He represents change and strife. He also opens the channel for all the

In the ancient kingdom of Abomey, many myths tell the story of the creation. The Yoruba believed that the sky and the earth formed a couple, Obatala and Odudua, represented by

the union of two half calabashes; the sculpture at the top places them on the heads of humans. Their union produced the gods, intended to serve the earthly world. One of them is Gu (left), the god of iron and fire, always shown with an axe in hand, as that is the emblem of thunder. In Benin, those who worship diligently at the convents are called 'fetishers'. The 'fetishers' (opposite) – also called 'daughters of the gods' – carry the axe of thunder. The platter made from bombax wood (above) is dedicated to Fa.

other deities to reach humans. Placed at the entrance to temples and the houses of the heads of families, he is invoked at the beginning of every ceremony. All individuals have their own Legba, which help them to overcome difficulties they encounter in their lives.

Other *vodun,* such as Dambala Wèdo and Ayida Wèdo, both symbolized by the rainbow/snake, form a couple responsible for ensuring the link between thunder (the sky) and the sea and for helping their faithful secure prestige and material wealth.

The pantheon of Dahomian gods seems to be divided into three major classes. One refers to the sky. Hevioso is a family of spirits that represents thunder. Another refers to the earth, like Sakpata, who fights epidemics. The third belongs to the domain of war, such as Gu, the god of iron, who carries a sword as his attribute and symbolizes both war and work, and Agwe, *vodun* of fishing. Benin holds to the existence of a supreme being, a female, called Mawu. She has a twin brother, Lisa, from whom

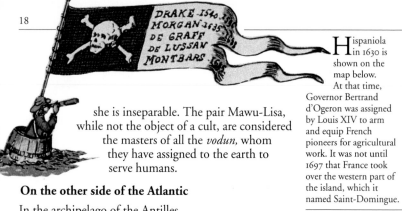

she is inseparable. The pair Mawu-Lisa, while not the object of a cult, are considered the masters of all the *vodun,* whom they have assigned to the earth to serve humans.

Hispaniola in 1630 is shown on the map below. At that time, Governor Bertrand d'Ogeron was assigned by Louis XIV to arm and equip French pioneers for agricultural work. It was not until 1697 that France took over the western part of the island, which it named Saint-Domingue.

On the other side of the Atlantic

In the archipelago of the Antilles, Haiti – the name given to the island by the native Taino and Arawak to indicate its mountainous nature – became Hispaniola when it was taken by the Spanish in 1492.

The indigenous population, which stood at about 1.3 million at the beginning of the 16th century, was decimated by cruel treatment, illness, and forced labour in the gold mines. After fifteen years, only about sixty thousand remained.

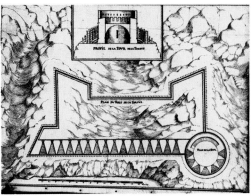

In 1503 the first cargo of slaves from Africa landed, brought in to replace native workers who showed the slightest disinclination to work in the mines. Then in 1517 Charles V authorized the importation of fifteen thousand black slaves.

The first small contingent of French travellers to settle the island of Tortuga, situated north of Haiti, landed in 1629. The group consisted of pirates, cattle rustlers and buccaneers who raided Spanish ships in the Caribbean Sea. Little by little, through fighting the Spanish, the French gained a foothold on the larger island, where they began to grow cacao, cotton and indigo. The French presence became so sizable that Louis XIV saw fit to name a French governor, Bertrand d'Ogeron, in 1665. The previous year, statesman and financier Jean-Baptiste Colbert had created the Compagnie des Indes to furnish the island with black slaves. In order to meet the pressing demands for labour, the company even imported impoverished whites, called *engagés,* who were treated like slaves for thirty-six months. Finally, in 1697, as a result of the Treaty of Ryswick, Spain ceded to

The impetus for Saint-Domingue's colonization came from pioneers who settled first on Tortuga Island. Buccaneers and pirates, they mostly traded in hides, which they took from wild cattle that they hunted and which also served as their source of food. Agriculture allowed them to stabilize their settlements, with the help of Bertrand d'Ogeron, former privateer and emissary of Louis XIV. France had other representatives in the Caribbean, including missionaries and the earliest plantation owners. But it was from Tortuga Island, to Hispaniola's northwest, that the French, after driving out the English, gradually succeeded in challenging Spain's hold on Hispaniola. Above, the fort of Tortuga Island, which was instrumental in the fierce fighting between Europeans.

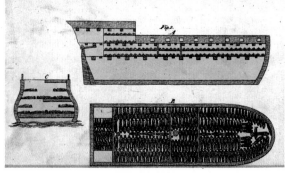

At the beginning of the 18th century, the slave trade of black Africans greatly increased and the slave ships were built larger. The holds were crowded with slaves, chained together in pairs. These ships were called 'floating tombs', as many slaves perished in the course of the forty to ninety days it took to reach Saint-Domingue. They were poorly fed and harshly treated in order to prevent any attempt at rebellion. Torn from their families and their kinship groups, the slaves experienced a profound sense of alienation.

France a third of the island, which took the name Saint-Domingue.

Guinea, mythical Africa

At that time, the first plantations were already producing sugar. A great transformation was taking hold of the process of sugar production due to the use of slave labour. During the 18th century, the slave trade reached its apex before diminishing, according to the expression of the period, due to a total 'Negro shortage'.

Most of the African peoples were represented in Saint-Domingue. But, of the three largest groups – the Sudanese, Guineans and Bantus – the one that carried the greatest influence was the Fon tribe of Dahomey, combined with the Yoruba of Nigeria, which provided the unifying basis for the ensemble of cultural practices transplanted to the island by the slaves.

Throughout the 17th century and, especially, in the first half of the 18th, the royal family of Dahomey ruled over several small kingdoms on the West African coast. It took from them numerous captives, and supplying the slave trade became the central pillar of its economy. Among the slaves could be found sorcerers, criminals and high priests of the *vodun* cult.

The slaves, dispatched from the Gulf of Guinea, knew that they had been sold by their own people, as attested by the Creole saying 'Depi lan Ginen, nèg rayi nèg' (Already in Guinea, the Negro hated the Negro). But Guinea was also considered the true birthplace of the spirits, and voodoo was kept alive as a last link with the lost ancestral home of Africa.

Baptism brings a new identity

Everything conspired to break down the African culture. Starting with the journey to the New World, the slaves were chained in pairs, regularly beaten and always poorly fed, to ensure that they had no strength to revolt. Then, once arrived on the island, they were given new names, from

African kings traded slaves for arms, pearls or alcohol (below, slave merchants in Gorée). The people they sold were prisoners of war or alleged criminals. In the 17th century, slave traffic in Africa was concentrated north of Sierra Leone and the islands of Cape Verde and, in the 18th century, on the Gold Coast and in Dahomey. After 1750 the slave trade was supplied by the kingdoms of Congo and Angola. In three centuries, between eleven and fifteen million black slaves were removed from Africa.

A priest baptizing slaves, from the Haitian point of view (detail from a 1983 painting by Rose-Marie Desruisseaux). Below, two slaves going for their baptism in a sentimental European version. Baptism, thought to strengthen the institution of slavery, actually reinforced voodoo's system of beliefs. Seeing in baptism a way to increase their magical powers, the slaves got baptized from three to six times. Their masters, suspecting the missionaries of preaching the doctrine of equality between blacks and whites, did what they could to avoid religious instruction for slaves.

mythology (e.g., Cupid, Zeus) or Roman history (e.g., Brutus, Pompey), according to the plantation owner's whimsy.

As they were distributed among the plantations, work groups (called *ateliers*), and huts, the different ethnic groups were systematically mixed;

in effect, slaves were meant to lose all memory of family, lineage and origins. Stripped of their humanity, they became easy to manage, primed for a life of total submission. They could not hold meetings and assemblies except under the watchful eye of the master.

The only permissible religion was Catholicism, which had even served to justify the slave trade and slavery. Louis XIII had stipulated, when the Compagnie Française des Iles d'Amérique was created in 1635 to carry on the slave trade, that the slaves they took had to be baptized and instructed in the Catholic religion. According to Father Jean-Baptiste Dutertre, one of the first missionaries active in Saint-Domingue, from 1640 to 1647, the conversion of the black people had been given as the fundamental goal of the commerce in human beings.

Evangelism as the rationalization for slavery

The Code Noir, or Black Code, prepared in France at the behest of Colbert and promulgated by Louis XIV in 1685, gives precise information on how the official justification for slavery fell on the Church. Article 2 stipulates, 'All the slaves in our islands will be baptized and instructed in the Catholic religion, apostolic and Roman'. And Article 3 insists, 'The public practice of all religion except Catholicism is forbidden....'

The Code was equally careful to outlaw any gathering of slaves, night or day, to prevent the practice of African religious traditions. It regulated every activity of the slaves – work, rest, family – and classed them as personal property, leaving them no rights.

Father Dutertre wrote concerning the slaves, 'Their servitude is the principle of their happiness and their misfortune the cause of their salvation'. Above, the frontispiece of his book *Histoire générale des Antilles habitées par les Français* (1667), which gives one of the earliest accounts of the slaves' daily life in Saint-Domingue, Guadeloupe and Martinique.

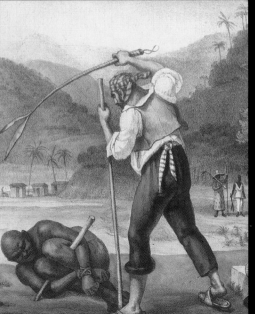

The habitations

Saint-Domingue's plantations dependent on slavery were each composed of a group of habitations (properties of about twenty-five acres), in which both agricultural and manufactory work was carried on. Each was autonomous in economic and administrative terms. At the centre of the area was the mill, run by wind, water or mules; beyond that were placed the buildings in which sugar was refined, the distillery, the blacksmith, the cooper's shed and the storehouses; then the slave quarters, the cattle pens, the chapel and the hospital. There were ten black people for every white in the habitations.

Récolte et Plantation de coton
eu temps de la Colonie

An implacable system

Slaves on Saint-Domingue worked from dawn to dusk, under the eye of a driver who acted as the master's right arm. He always carried a whip or a club to punish recalcitrant slaves. At first the drivers were white people, former indentured servants in the colony, but from the beginning of the 18th century their jobs were given to black people, who cost less to keep. They had to wake the slaves up in the morning, assign them their tasks and give reports to the masters of everything that occurred on the habitation. The very small number of domestic slaves enjoyed a privileged life compared with the fate of slaves in the work groups and on the plantations.

Two seasons coexist in this landscape: *The Gathering* (left) *and Planting of Cotton* (right) *in Colonial Times*, a painting by Eddy Jacques. In the middle ground, crossing the wide path, a master visits the scene of his exploitation in comfort, carried by two domestic slaves.

Among the sixty articles making up the Black Code, not a single one calls for the mitigation of the terrible treatment suffered by the slave. All of its references to rest, nourishment or religion aim at the prevention of flight and give the master absolute control. In theory, the owner could be severely punished for treating his slave badly, but slaves were forbidden to be summoned as witnesses in the courts, either civil or criminal.

At work as in religious affairs, slaves were constantly threatened by the whip of the *commandeur,* or driver, and of the manager and the overseer, all of whom were invariably white, themselves under the orders of the *procureur,* or agent, to whom the plantation owner, in his frequent absences, delegated his authority.

Homo sum; humani nihil a me alienum puto.
Je suis Homme; et rien de ce qui intéresse l'Homme ne m'est étranger

As a reaction to being violently torn from their roots, to having their every word and gesture controlled, and, to having Christianity forced on them, the slaves tried to resume their cultural and religious traditions. These represented a force – at once individual and collective – for their survival. Ancestral spirits, forces called supernatural, were invoked and celebrated in secret, far from the masters' eyes yet in the shadow of the Church, as the worship of saints and the Catholic sacraments served as a screen and a support for African beliefs.

The Black Code of 1685 legislated the rights of the white masters. Even in 1791 (engraving above), while revolt rocked Saint-Domingue, most humanists could only envision a gradual abolition of slavery.

'An ancient idolatrous cult' – Father Labat

The masters, administrators and missionaries misread the significance of the emergence of voodoo. They ascribed any African beliefs or practices to superstition, idolatry or satanism, if they did not simply consider them signs of infantilism or madness.

Father Labat, who at the end of the 17th century provided one of the earliest accounts of the religious life of slaves in Saint-Domingue, believed sorcery to be the natural bent of 'the Negroes'. He wrote, 'Before baptizing the adults, it is necessary to mark out those who filled the role of sorcerer in their country, for whatever promises they make they will rarely abandon them'. If voodoo was vaguely noticed, it was only to enforce its interdiction. Periodic arrests, regulations and reports served as reminders that the magic practices that slaves used to help cure them of sickness were repressed by fines and corporal punishment.

The first description of voodoo to approach reality came from the French traveller Moreau de Saint-Méry in 1797. Even he, like the missionaries, did not refrain from condemning the ceremony he managed to attend as 'a kind of Bacchanalia' that gave way to 'a disgusting prostitution'.

He noted that the slaves were 'Arada Negroes', that is, from the town of Allada in Dahomey, who lived by the beliefs and rules of voodoo. Worship consisted of dances performed around a snake from which the faithful gained the power to know the past and

In his book *Voyage aux Isles de l'Amérique*, Father Labat describes life on the plantations. A sugar planter as well as a missionary, he admitted having thrashed slaves, whom he took for sorcerers, to death for practising African religions. 'A writer curious about countries and behaviour, [he] chastises man and his faults while maintaining a cheerful tone, and knows how to blend throughout the agreeable and the useful', claims a caption below the engraving.

the future. Ceremonies took place at night, in the greatest of secrecy. The initiates twined red handkerchiefs around their bodies and presented offerings to a 'snake' in a box enclosed with wire set on an altar. After greetings were given to the priest, a goat was sacrificed and its blood poured on the participants, who swore to remain faithful to the cult. All were then immediately overcome by nervous agitation and spun around until they fell to the ground.

Return to the source and new contributions

Moreau de Saint-Méry alluded to trance and 'possession'. However, he touched on only one aspect of voodoo: a specific religion practised by one of the royal families of Dahomey that worshipped the *vodun* Dambala Wèdo, represented by a rainbow/snake.

In Saint-Domingue, where there were fewer ties to a royal aristocracy, the slaves restored the religion to a diverse family of spirits, called nations, or *nanchon*. The spirits were no longer referred to as *vodu* or *vodun* but as *lwa, mistè* (mysteries), *zanj* (angels) or saints, according to the region of the country. An entirely new mythology arose and thrived at the core of the slaves' lives, due partly to contacts that had developed among different peoples and partly to the contributions from the culture of the surviving Carib Indians, from Christianity and from Freemasonry.

Until the 18th century, the earliest descriptions of voodoo were dominated by stereotypes of a religion considered as snake-worshipping, diabolical and barbarous. Its power to lend cultural cohesion to the slaves, its language of stability and control, the wealth of its myths and its rites went unnoticed by outside observers. Nonetheless, planters and officials already perceived its secret and mysterious character as a danger to the system of slavery.

Moreau de Saint-Méry served as president of the electors of Paris in July 1789. In 1797 he published the first volume of his work entitled *Description topographique, physique, civile, politique et historique de la partie française de l'Isle de Saint-Domingue*, which gave a detailed description of the rites and beliefs of the black slaves.

As far as the Europeans at the beginning of the 18th century were concerned, African religions did not exist. The worship of Indians and Africans in Hispaniola could be explained only as satanism. The engraving opposite shows 'a religious ceremony of the natives of the Spanish Isle', from *L'Histoire générale des cérémonies* by B. Picart (1673–1733).

Oppressed by a system of slavery intent on effacing their humanity, black people uprooted from Africa slowly evolved their own religion, based on the rites of voodoo. It created a communal bond that served as the secret foundation for their various struggles for freedom.

CHAPTER 2

VOODOO HIDDEN IN THE HELL OF SLAVERY

Baptism introduced slaves to their new condition, but it also gave them an opening for the rituals of voodoo. The detail of a painting by Rose-Marie Desruisseaux (opposite) illustrates slaves dancing at nightfall, when the African spirits recover their strength. Freed slaves (right) rejected the nudity of their former status and copied their former masters instead.

The system of slavery set up in the New World differed totally from that already practised in Africa, which was limited to domestic work. Originally prisoners of war, slaves in the kingdom of Dahomey were considered almost members of the family, even while retaining the status of strangers lacking blood ties with their masters. However, once they were sold on the international market, they became articles of merchandise. Their buyers sought to wring from them the greatest possible profit, even if it meant exhausting them completely. In Saint-Domingue, the average slave lasted only seven to ten years. The masters knew that they could easily replace this perishable labour, thanks to the slave trade.

Adaptation: the recovery of African beliefs

Guillaume Bosman, employed by the Dutch West India Company, wrote in 1705, 'The poor innocents think that we buy and transport them only for the purpose of fattening them up and then making a good meal of them'. Indeed, slaves considered slavers and planters to be cannibals or sorcerers who had at their call spirit forces more powerful than those in Africa,

Representing the extreme left in the French Constituent Assembly in 1790, Abbé Grégoire fought for the abolition of slavery in the colonies and the equality of black and white people in the churches. These illustrations from his *Manuel de piété pour les Noirs* (1820, left) display his willingness to banish discrimination in conferring the sacraments.

since they succeeded in wresting them away. They also believed that they could rejoin the world of their ancestors through suicide, leaving only their body to the white masters.

How could the slaves adapt to the harsh conditions in the work groups and on the plantations and at the same time overcome the imposed isolation? The prohibition on the practice of their African religious traditions was undermined by the requirement that they follow Christianity. Therefore, slaves surrounded their African beliefs with the protective covering of the adoration of saints, the sacraments, the processions and all the great liturgical holidays.

Throughout the period of slavery, and wherever the colonials settled, missionaries could also be found. From 1704 to 1764, the northern part of Saint-Domingue became a fiefdom of the Jesuits. They built the church of Cap-François (below) and created the role of 'priest to the Negroes' to evangelize the slaves in segregated masses – held well away from those of the whites.

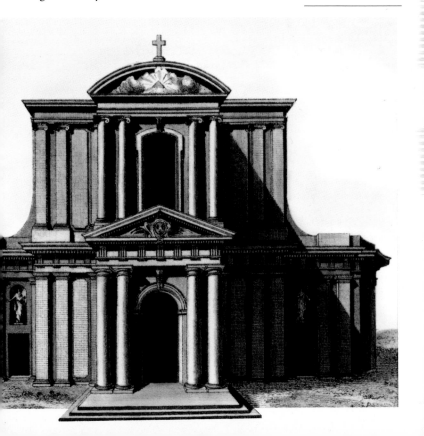

Missionaries and officials had long denounced 'the dances and gatherings of Negroes' accompanied by the sound of the drums, which could give way to uprisings and rebellions. Restricted in their practices by regulations and ordinances, the slaves hid voodoo under cover of Catholic ceremonies. At first deceived by the religious

fervour demonstrated by their slaves, the masters finally noticed that it was not innocent in nature and henceforth kept a close guard on their enthusiasm for Catholicism.

Escape: the runaway slave

The second form of resistance slaves had was to establish their own turf, which could serve not only as a hiding place but also as a base of operations against the institution of slavery. The ultimate goal was to win freedom, by finding their way to places where the master could not follow.

Slaves began fleeing work groups and plantations as early as the 16th century. As the number of slaves imported vastly increased, the incidence of runaways seemed to reach epidemic proportions, in spite of all efforts to thwart it.

Driven by hunger, harsh treatment or simply the thirst for freedom, runaways,

Slaves who fled the plantations were pursued by dogs specially imported from Europe for that purpose. But nothing could stop them. Their numbers increased and they developed and structured their fugitive existence.

known as Maroons, headed towards the Bahoruco Mountains (in the southwest part of today's Dominican Republic), where they met up with others and formed a new community, an economic, political and cultural entity. Maroons generally arrived with their own farming tools, and sometimes even the horse or mule that was in their care.

Without the network of contacts in the work groups or among domestic slaves, Maroons had a very hard time

Hidden in the mountains and in caves, the Maroons developed close bonds of solidarity. The painting above suggests the difficulty and insecurity of their new life, with its freedom but need for secrecy.

surviving, as the agricultural yield in the mountains did not come close to feeding everyone. They returned from time to time to make forays against the settlements. If caught, they were severely punished – their ears were cut off, they were pilloried, burned, and so on – none of which prevented them from attempting to escape again or kept others from escaping.

By 1750 there were close to three thousand Maroons in Saint-Domingue. If captured, the runaway was severely punished and imprisoned (left and below).

Voodoo in the mountains

The runaway camps were mostly populated by the least acculturated slaves, that is, the *bossales,* or the fresh arrivals, as opposed to the Creoles, slaves born in the colony who were used to the daily life. Thus, African principles of organization came easily in the fabrication of a new culture that was differentiated from that of the masters.

Dances, songs, mythology, rituals, medicinal treatments, as well as the development of the Creole language and a new family organization based on African

kinship structures combined to forge new bonds
between the slaves who had run away. Voodoo fostered
a sense of common identity among slaves of different
ethnic backgrounds and from different plantations.
Before being accepted into the community, every
new runaway had to swear not to betray his or her
companions if captured. The oath was taken in

front of the camp's leader, who often was the
voodoo priest as well.

In the community, the revival of African
traditions carried a specific objective: the
suppression of slavery. Thus the runaway
slave learned to employ all the resources of
magic and sorcery, guided by the voodoo
priests, who were as skilful at making
charms as at utilizing poisonous plants and
deadly potions.

François Makandal, leader and sorcerer

From 1750 to 1791, Saint-Domingue's slave
masters lived in fear. Many of their number
had died of poisoning. The voodoo spirits
seemed to have extraordinary powers that
baffled the colonial police. Despite the
prohibition on the making and selling of
suspicious drugs as well as on the practice of

In order to head off any
attempts at rebellion,
the official punishment
of executing captured
Maroons in public was
often followed, with free
black people, whites
and other slaves in
attendance. Above,
soldiers of the colonial
army take their positions
for the execution of three
Maroons.

African magic, the unseen power of voodoo was so terrifying that it succeeded in attacking the very foundation of the slave system.

On the colonial scene appeared Maroon leaders, known for their 'magic' powers, who prophesied the extermination of the whites and the liberation of the slaves. Some of these became genuine politicians and developed a coherent plan to win independence. One of the best known, in 1757, was François Makandal. He sowed the seeds of fear among the planters and officials, not only by concocting poisons that killed slowly but also by obtaining talismans, called *garde-corps* (literally, body-guards), for rebellious slaves; the talismans were said to make them invulnerable to weapons and free them of all fear of white people. Later, *makandal* became a general designation for talismans and poisons made in Saint-Domingue.

For several years Makandal, a Muslim from Guinea, prophesied the extermination of the white masters. He spread terror among them with the threat of secret poisons. He was said to have several groups of Maroons under his control. Arrested in 1758 and condemned to be burned at the stake, he managed to leap free of the fire. The painting above illustrates the feat of the 'rebellious slave with magical powers' in front of the church of Cap-François, who stupefies the spectators.

On the eve of the French Revolution in 1789, the colonials led a luxurious and apparently tranquil life. They are shown on the left strolling in the port of Nippes, in the south of Saint-Domingue. Attached to the privileges of birth, they seem oblivious to what visitors already called 'a veritable volcano' beneath their dancing feet.

The privileged life of Saint-Domingue's planters

At the end of the 18th century, the colony had 400,000 to 500,000 slaves, 40,000 whites and 25,000 free black people and mulattoes. At the time, Saint-Domingue was responsible for over a third of the trade outside France, making it the richest of its colonies. Every year, 500 ships unloaded sugar, coffee, indigo, copper and wood in the mother country's ports. In 1789, Saint-Domingue had 793 sugar plantations.

If, however, France viewed Saint-Domingue as a major economic resource, the whites who lived there, whether the so-called *petit blanc* (employee or petty functionary) or *grand blanc* (plantation owner, royal official or merchant), were interested only in their own affairs. Their daily life revolved around dinner parties and balls; their disputes centred on the managers' mistresses, often mulattoes. Their taverns, roadhouses and theatres were all packed to overflowing.

In the mid-18th century, several Masonic lodges were established on the island, and they brought with them notions of tolerance and secularization. Freedmen, including some black people, joined the brotherhood, however, planters took care that the Masonic doctrines did not enjoy much success. In other

Although he was retaken and executed soon after his startling escape from the flames, Makandal continued to haunt the masters and administrators for some time. His name was lent to poisons, to talismans and to certain ceremonies in which magic charms that rendered their owners invulnerable were made. The sheet-metal cutout below recalls such acts of sorcery.

respects, the relationship with France had always been considered constraining, because of the law of 'exclusive trade', which would not permit the sale of colonial goods to any country but France and which set all the prices. Thus, the winds of rebellion – even among the planters themselves – never ceased to blow on Saint-Domingue.

The ceremony of Bois-Caïman

All the prohibitions of voodoo ceremonies and *makandals* came to nothing as the slave population learned of the French Revolution and the Declaration of the Rights of Man. They realized the moment was auspicious to lead a final attack against slavery. The new Maroon leader, a man named Boukman Dutty, was a former slave *commandeur* and coachman familiar with many work groups. He was also a voodoo priest. From the Lenormand de Mézy plantation – the same as

Even today, the ceremony of Bois-Caïman (above, evoked in a painting by Dieudonné Cédor) lives in the Haitian imagination as a seminal event.

Makandal's – he gave the signal to revolt to all the Maroon camps, as well as to the slaves in the work groups and plantations in the northern part of the colony.

The accounts of planters and parish priests lead one to believe that a revolt was carefully planned in great secrecy. A first meeting between the leaders of the Maroon camps led to a second, framed by a voodoo ceremony presided over by Boukman, on 14 August 1791.

From accounts that freely mix fact and legend it emerges that during this ceremony, called Bois-Caïman, the assembled slaves sealed a sacred pact, swearing to die rather than live under the foot of the colonial masters. Participants shared the blood of a sacrificed black pig while Boukman, speaking in Creole, called for vengeance in the name of the gods of their African ancestors and in defiance of the god of the white people. The insurrection began on August 22.

The new Spartacus

For two months, the rebellious slaves spread terror throughout the colony.

Since Makandal conceived the idea of exterminating the whites in 1757, the slaves in the north waited for the right moment to launch an assault against slavery. After many extremely secret meetings, a group of rebel leaders led by Boukman, a slave from Jamaica and coachman from a plantation in the north, organized an assembly of representatives from work groups and plantations in order to clinch the plans for insurrection. On the night of 14 August 1791 (22 August according to some historians), in a thick forest in an area called Bois-Caïman in the hills overlooking the town of Cap Haitien, the undertaking was sealed with a voodoo ceremony.

News of the slave rebellion of 1791 quickly made its way to Europe through colonials who managed to escape. Their stories reinforced the image of 'savage Negroes, cruel and barbaric', avid for revenge and blood, slaughtering or raping white women, setting fire to plantations and driving colonials to flight. On the left is a German version of these events in an engraving of 1792.

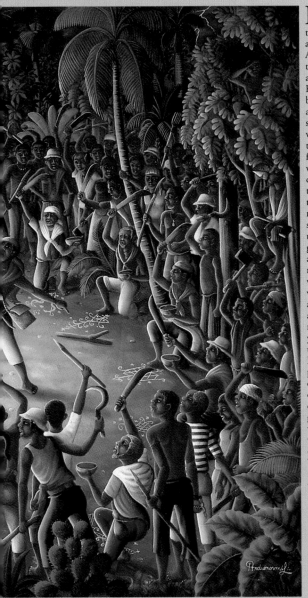

It was a stormy night. The wind blew through the trees and the atmosphere was tense. A young priestess, traditionally identified as a mulatto named Cécile Fatiman, sacrificed a black pig. Dancing, with a large knife in her hand, she sang African songs, which were taken up by the others. The blood from the animal's throat was collected and distributed among all as they swore a solemn oath to keep their planned rebellion the deepest secret. Boukman, the uncontested leader of the group, rose, invoked God and exhorted the slaves to revenge: 'The Good Lord who created the sun which lights us from above, which stirs the sea and makes the thunder roar – listen well, all of you – this god, hidden in the clouds, watches us. He sees what the white people do. The god of the white people demands from them crimes; our god asks for good deeds. But this god who is so good demands vengeance! He will direct our hands; he will aid us. Throw away the image of the god of the whites, who thirsts for our tears, and listen to the voice of liberty that speaks in all of our hearts!' Here is the mythical ceremony as imagined by André Normil.

Two hundred sugar plantations and 1800 coffee plantations went up in flames; about a thousand white people were killed. Boukman died in an ambush. Among the new leaders who emerged was Toussaint-Louverture, grandson of the king of the Arada. Born on the Breda plantation, in the northern part of the island, he, too, had been a coachman. He also knew how to read and write. He had heard about Abbé Raynal's *Histoire des deux Indes* (History of the Two Indies), which predicted the appearance of a new Spartacus on Saint-Domingue who would free the black people.

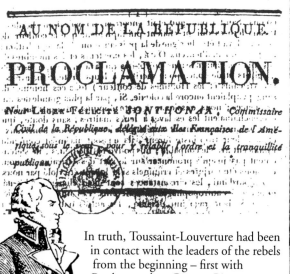

In truth, Toussaint-Louverture had been in contact with the leaders of the rebels from the beginning – first with Boukman, then Georges Biassou, Jeannot Bullet and Jean-François, whose secretary he would become. Gradually, his name became widely known and he gained considerable authority, not only with the mulattoes but also with the white colonials. A true military genius, he forged his own army of five hundred men and elected at first to ally himself with the Spanish, who still controlled the

Sonthonax (left) was one of three members of the civil commission sent by France to reestablish order in the colony after the slave rebellion. After abolishing the Colonial Assembly of the whites, he broke away from the expeditionary corps that accompanied him.

eastern part of the island, abandoning them when necessary to protect the freedom of the black people. He turned instead to the white royalists, as he believed that Louis XVI desired to abolish slavery. His army quickly swelled its ranks, reaching five thousand men.

On 29 August 1793, Léger Félicité Sonthonax, former lawyer of the Parisian Assembly and known for his revolutionary sympathies, declared the universal abolition of slavery. He and two others had been sent by the National Convention, the ruling body of the French government

Suspected of being pro-abolitionist, Sonthonax was deported to France, but he first distributed arms among the slaves (illustrated above in a painting by Eddy Jacques), and inspired thousands of whites to flee to the United States.

after the revolution, to make peace. The result confirmed the victory of the rebellion of August 1791.

Toussaint-Louverture: the price of black power

Taking advantage of a weakened France caught in the midst of revolution, England invaded Saint-Domingue. It won the help of the French colonials with its avowed wish to reinstate slavery. Toussaint-Louverture succeeded in pushing them out and was rewarded by being named major-general under the French flag. Bolstered by the confidence of the black populace, he reorganized work and discipline on the plantations, collaborating with those planters who accepted the end of slavery. Safeguarding the freedom of the black people remained his strategy and his goal.

In 1801, after conquering the Spanish part of the island, where he himself declared the end of slavery, Toussaint-Louverture put forward a constitution that established Saint-Domingue's independence from France and that proclaimed him governor-general for life. In 1802 Napoleon sent an expeditionary force to reestablish colonial rule. But he was too late: Toussaint-Louverture, although deported to France and imprisoned in the Joux fortress, where he died, had had the time to lay the groundwork for independence. Freedmen joined the slaves to put a halt to Napoleon's army in a war led by new black and mulatto generals, Jean-Jacques Dessalines, Alexandre Pétion and Henri Christophe. Its independence confirmed on 1 January 1804, the country went back to its old name: Haiti.

Voodoo and international respectability

What would become of voodoo in the newly independent state? How would the new political leaders and the new elite deal with their African heritage – which had played a large role in gaining them power – with all of Europe, wearing the blinkers of its colonial ideology, seeing itself as the saviour of an Africa given

The expression 'beat the drum' has long been associated with celebrating the voodoo religion. The main instrument in voodoo worship, the drum calls up the spirits of African Guinea and of the ancestors. It is considered a divinity whose energy must be renewed through specific rites; baptized with a special ceremony, it receives offerings of food and libations. The drum on the left is one of those called *asòtò*; about 1.38 metres high, it dates from 1806 and is said to have been used in the war of independence. Each time the Church or the state went on the offensive against paganism, these instruments were burned and their use forbidden.

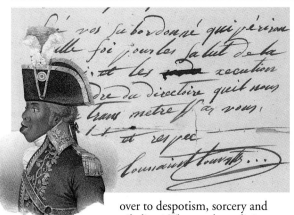

over to despotism, sorcery and cannibalism? The voodoo religion has no written basis; it has no dogma nor a centralized organization, much less a set ritual. It would be hard for it to attain the status of an official religion. The earliest heads of government – Toussaint-Louverture, Dessalines, Pétion, Christophe – even tried to reduce the influence of voodoo priests with a campaign of persecution. They understood the advantage of adopting Catholicism as the official religion, thinking it would place them on an equal footing with the European nations.

On becoming governor-general of the island, Toussaint-Louverture (left, his portrait and a letter of 1793 to the Naval Minister carrying his signature) exercised absolute power. He believed a federation of the island with France to be possible, but he remained inflexible on the abolition of slavery and Saint-Domingue's autonomy. His deportation in 1802 to France strengthened the resolve of the slaves to lead a war for independence. The troops of General Leclerc, sent by Napoleon in response to entreaties by colonists eager to regain their properties, fell victim as much to yellow fever as to combat (below).

VOODOO

Rada Drums

Sacrificial Goat

Maman Julie—
Voodoo Priestess.

In the eyes of Westerners in the 19th century, any element of African culture smacked of barbarism. In Haiti, the agitators who emerged from the rebellion of 1791 and the revolution were used as proof of a connection between voodoo and savagery. The same apprehension was invoked in the 20th century to justify the American occupation of Haiti in 1915, turning the island into something seen as a land of the living dead.

CHAPTER 3

CAMPAIGNS AGAINST SORCERY

In his book *The White King of La Gonave* (1931), Lt Faustin Wirkus illustrated the symbols of barbarism as viewed by US Marines in Haiti (opposite). Above, he poses behind the ritual drums of voodoo; centre, a tree in which the 'spirits' reside, from which a sacrificed goat hangs; below, a priestess in front of the peristyle of her temple.

President of Haiti for life from 1818 to 1843, Jean-Pierre Boyer (right) is chiefly known for his rural code, which from 1826 to today has consigned the Haitian peasant to a marginal existence, and for the penal code of 1835, which classified voodoo under the label 'superstitions' and made its practice illegal, subject to fines and imprisonment.

Numerous Catholic priests in the northern part of the country took part in the movement for independence, preaching the right to revolt against the masters and serving as negotiators between the rebel leaders and the colonials. Some of these priests accepted the new civil constitution, which sought to bring the Church under the jurisdiction of the government, although this measure was rejected by the Vatican. After 1797, in accordance with the Declaration of the Rights of Man, Abbé Grégoire sent constitutionally ordained missionaries to Toussaint-Louverture.

A satanic image nourished by tales of travellers

Meanwhile, the voodoo religion of independent Haiti held the attention of European observers. The French traveller Paul Dormoys reported that, just as in 1791, voodoo continued to wreak havoc in the Haitian countryside. He wrote that they still used 'the bodies of wretches that they were able to get hold of for these dreadful banquets aimed at forcing the sun away'.

Now, however, they no longer had the excuse of avenging the master. Not only were they inferior in his opinion, 'Negroes' were also openly displaying their perverseness. Racist ideology, on the rise in the 19th century, found in voodoo an inexhaustible source of fodder.

In 1850 Haiti's head of state, Faustin Soulouque, an ardent follower of voodoo, made himself

Europe cast a jaundiced eye on Faustin Soulouque, the Haitian emperor. The newspapers declared him 'the sum of all the reminiscences of aboriginal savagery' and claimed that he had set Haiti on a course of 'full regression to African barbarism'. Daumier's 1850 caricature (opposite) shows him, dressed in his imperial garb, about to drop a journalist who dared to criticize Haitian politics into boiling water.

Europeans saw the rebellious slaves of 1791 as horrible fanatics inspired by sorcerers. They were supposed to have taken their vengeance by eating the hearts and livers of white people they captured after having drunk the blood of a black pig.

emperor and imposed an implacable dictatorship. After his fall in 1860, Haiti signed an agreement with the Vatican establishing Catholicism as the official religion of all Haitians. Henceforth, the Church periodically led campaigns of persecution against voodoo. It retreated

into secrecy, only to be dragged back into public notice by a scandalous rumour spread by the newspapers. In 1881 a former British consul, Spencer St John, declared that voodoo, attended by cannibalism and human sacrifice, was the main reason for the regression of Haitian civilization.

Premature independence in a land ruled by superstition

Several years later, American authors, such as Heskett Pritchard in 1910, took up the slack, discovering voodoo in their turn. Alluding to the attachment of the upper class and intellectual elite to the French language and culture, Haiti was described as 'a strange graft of Parisianism and savagery'. Dominated as they are by superstition, these American authors said, the black people have proved incapable of governing themselves. In addition, they do not stop at sacrificing chickens in their voodoo ceremonies; they accompany

The main problem encountered by Americans during the occupation of Haiti from 1915 to 1934 was the 'pacification' of the peasants. Often forced into hard labour on the roads, thousands of peasants were massacred, while many in the north were sent to a concentration camp at Chalbert. Above, a victorious Marine poses after an armed confrontation with rebels. When the Americans left in 1934, 'civilizing' the country was left to the police, a brutal heritage of the occupation.

A bove and below, the beginning and end of the occupation. On 28 July 1915, the *Washington* cast anchor in Port-au-Prince and its troops came ashore, illustrated above in a detail from a painting by Franz Augustin; below, a Marine photographed with some Haitian children at the market-place of Gonaïves before his departure in 1934.

these sacrifices with what were called 'kids without horns' – that is, babies. Such horror stories took deep root in the perceived 'character of the race'.

These characterizations led to the belief that independence came prematurely to Haiti and that the black people still had need of the whites' guidance in order to take their place among civilized nations. The clear link among race, voodoo and despotism in American public opinion paved the way for the American occupation of Haiti.

In 1915 US Marines landed in the guise of liberators to begin an occupation that would last until 1934. They prided themselves on

all the wonderful things they were doing for Haiti, such as pillaging the voodoo temples and destroying the 'idols' of the African ancestors.

Sensations and sanctions

In his book *The White King of La Gonave,* which became famous at the beginning of this period in the United States, then in Europe, and even in Japan, selling ten million copies, Lt Faustin Wirkus, a Marine, gave an account of the damage he inflicted in order to 'save' the Haitian people from cannibalism and black magic. As far as he was concerned, the *cacos,* or protesters against the American occupation, were practitioners of voodoo.

THE
WHITE KING
OF
LA GONAVE

WIRKUS AND DUDLEY

Other books, with such suggestive titles as *Cannibal Cousins,* painted a picture of Haiti as the land of 'zombies', for voodoo, it was reported, had the strange custom of 'reviving the dead'. The zombie and 'voodoo death' gradually became a favourite theme of American horror films. All these stories claimed as their foundation the complaints and evidence brought forward at Haitian tribunals

Lt Faustin Wirkus (above), who seems to have penetrated the ranks of voodoo followers (top), recounted his exploits in *The White King of La Gonave,* published in 1931: 'We had orders from head-quarters, as the natives well knew, to make a report leading to criminal punitive action on all *papalois, hougans, bocors* and *mamalois* or as the orders read: "on all voodoo artists". Officially we were informed that the voodoo cult was the medium of black magic....'

La religion Catholique Persecute le Vodoo (Campagne des rejetes)

and, especially, the article of the penal code that since 1835 had exacted fines and imprisonment of those who created zombies or cast spells. Pushed into secrecy, the voodoo priests themselves were forced to adopt a strategy to surround worship with mystery and reinforce their own power. While carrying out repeated 'antisuperstition campaigns' (1864, 1896, 1912, 1925–30, 1940–1), the government and the Church came together to destroy temples, burn cult objects and imprison the *oungan,* or voodoo priests. The campaign of 1940–1 enjoined every Catholic to declare in public an 'oath of rejection', which consisted of renouncing voodoo practices, recognized as a satanic cult.

The 'antisuperstitious' campaign of 1941 sought to eradicate voodoo. Thousands of Catholics publicly took an oath which consisted of renouncing voodoo forever as a form of satanism. Assisted by the army, the priests went on horseback to attack the voodoo temples and set huge bonfires of objects sacred to voodoo. Above, a painting by Eddy Jacques depicts one of these attacks.

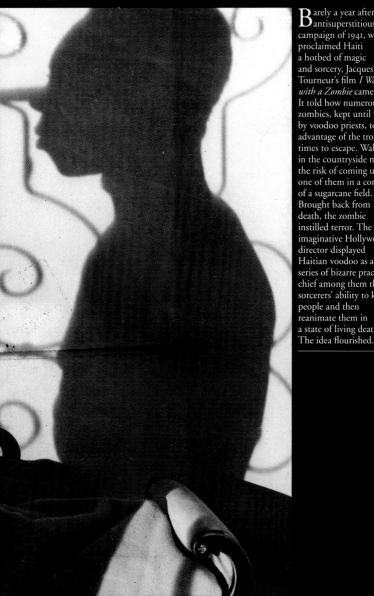

Barely a year after the antisuperstitious campaign of 1941, which proclaimed Haiti a hotbed of magic and sorcery, Jacques Tourneur's film *I Walked with a Zombie* came out. It told how numerous zombies, kept until then by voodoo priests, took advantage of the troubled times to escape. Walking in the countryside meant the risk of coming upon one of them in a corner of a sugarcane field. Brought back from death, the zombie instilled terror. The imaginative Hollywood director displayed Haitian voodoo as a series of bizarre practices, chief among them the sorcerers' ability to kill people and then reanimate them in a state of living death. The idea flourished.

'Wanga', 'baka' and werewolves

Some awkward semantic ambiguities lurk in the language of voodoo followers. For example, 'to eat someone' means to capture that individual's spirit through sorcery. Within its own network of beliefs and practices, voodoo has its own order, yet one that is antithetical to the Cartesian version of reality. In voodoo, the imagination knows no bounds.

Every believer is convinced that it is possible to capture supernatural forces, enclose them in bottles or packets, called *wanga,* and use the *wanga* to prepare and cast spells. Conflicts or rivalries between families, neighbours or friends from the same neighbourhood or village often give rise to the use of a *wanga.* It may employ defensive magic that does not lead to death. At the most, a *wanga* causes sickness or various setbacks. It has a limited sphere of action and applies only to the individual targeted.

Using a *baka,* a malevolent power

Wanga, or magic charms (below left), are fetishes that concentrate spiritual power in order to gain protection against spells – in defensive magic – or to attack one's enemies – in offensive magic. In the creation of *wanga,* songs and prayers always accompany the assembling of the various ingredients. The act of creation, as well as the resulting object, is called a *travail,* or labour.

that takes the form of a dwarf, a small monster or an animal, is another story. People who resort to them are taking a big risk, for the bloodthirsty *baka* may demand a member of their family in exchange for its services.

Other actions delve into the realm of sorcery and take aim at the progressive deterioration of the target. The 'werewolves' who devote themselves to this end are sorcerers, possessed by insatiable spirits, who are believed to turn themselves into animals in order to suck the blood of babies. The tendency to become a werewolf can be inherited, or it can be the result of the rash act of buying evil spirits.

Living without free will: the zombie

The most dreaded form of sorcery is the practice of creating zombies. Already 'dead' and buried, the zombie is reawakened to a semiconscious life to serve as a slave on a plantation. Only the *oungan* 'practising with both hands' (those voodoo priests who practise magic and sorcery) know the secret and the exact dose of poison to administer in order to make people appear dead and then revive them in the graves where they had been placed. Rumours of zombies

The protective spirit known as a *baka* or a *gad* (guard) can be delivered by a voodoo priest in the form of a dwarf (above). It protects a house or property. Believed to be evil, the *baka* can turn on its owner to inflict various misfortunes, including his or her death or the death of their loved ones.

A *bòkò*, or magician, accompanied by four initiates (left), sprinkles water from a bottle in his hand on the magic charms to win the protection of the spirits. All wear necklaces that represent the *pwen* (points), spiritual forces that make the individual invulnerable to evil spells.

seen in markets or in crowds periodically spread through the country.

According to popular belief, the making of a zombie depends on the capture of one of the individual's spirits. In that state, the zombie is aware of everything happening but does not have available the means to react; he is mentally directed by the *oungan* who bewitched him. A true living dead, he has listless eyes, a stiff walk and a nasal voice, all of which mark him as being of the 'other world'. It sometimes happens, it is said, that zombies regain consciousness and voluntarily return to their graves.

The fear of zombiism leads some families to ensure that their dead are truly dead by poisoning the bodies.

Hector Hyppolite, painter and initiate of voodoo, depicts two zombies freshly taken from their tombs and led by the *oungan* to the field where they will be set to work (above). The living-dead zombies are said to be conscious but deprived of will. Some people have declared themselves zombies, and others, it is said, may be found in the streets (left). The voodoo follower holds 'zombification' to be the supreme punishment, as it reduces the individual to a slave – precisely the condition against which voodoo developed.

Gangs and individuals of little integrity

Since colonial times, Haiti has had secret societies, offshoots or branches of institutions that are still current in Africa. According to the area of origination, they are called *zobop, vlenbendeng* or *champwel* (hairless). They meet at night and make the rounds of the village, functioning as sentinels.

Participants have a secret password and have made a dangerous commitment, it is said, which could mean giving up a family member. In return, they gain magic wealth and powers that make them invulnerable to sorcery. Those who come upon a gang from a secret society unexpectedly at a crossroads can be easily bewitched.

However, voodoo followers do not identify their religion with magic and witchcraft. This is the tendency of outsiders, who are fascinated by the seemingly 'realistic' accounts given by practitioners, who are walled in by a hierarchical conception of religious systems, and who give way to the temptation to project on to voodoo that which is repressed by their own culture.

From these factors arise the literary and cinematic fate of this sulphurous subject.

For those who live in it, voodoo is a symbolic system that works by means of principles and rules that can be ascertained as much by means of the 'mythology' that tells the story of the spirits (or *lwa*) as by the complex rituals and norms of behaviour available to the followers.

The passport of a secret society allows its holder to go out at night without fear of sorcery. These bands of sorcerers are imputed to be able to change into herds of goats, horses or cattle.

• Countless stories heard about *zobop* really belong to the province of the fairy-tale, but it seems likely that certain people do sometimes band together, in secret, to practise sorcery or to use the popular belief in sorcerer societies to sow terror around them.

Proof that the matter is not wholly a question of superstition is to be found in the passports of *zobop*, confiscated in *humfo* [temples] or handed over to priests by repentant voodooists.•

Alfred Métraux
Voodoo in Haiti, 1972

For the voodoo faithful, the belief in spirits mediates between them and the world, as well as between individuals. Each spirit, or *lwa,* can be likened to a word in a language; in itself, it has only a narrow meaning. The spirits gain their importance as an ensemble of families, working to complement or oppose each other, together forming the voodoo pantheon.

CHAPTER 4

THE SPIRIT OF THE 'LWA'

Both nearby and far away, the Great Master (opposite, painted by Hector Hyppolite) represents fate as well as providence and exercises absolute control over all creation. A *vèvè,* drawn on the ground with flour or coffee grounds, invokes the presence of the spirits. This one (right) shows the symbols of Ezili, the *lwa* of love, and Dambala, represented by the snakes.

The logic of fate

The *lwa* are supernatural beings that can enter the human body, and they are thought to be present in all realms of nature: in the trees, the streams and the mountains; in the air, the water and fire. This belief is foreign to a modern sensibility, which does not ascribe God's hand to all events and elements of nature.

The *lwa* of voodoo establish a web of linkages between human activities – agriculture, war, courtship – and various aspects of the natural world. They create the structure of time and space, and they take control of an individual's life from birth to death. It would seem that listening very carefully for their messages would enable the faithful to learn and realize their fates. The spirits

Intended to consecrate a place, the *vèvè* above combines the symbols of various *lwa*, including Ibo Lélé, guardian of customs and flags.

provide a way of classifying the different provinces of the universe, as well as of life in society. Order and disorder, life and death, good and evil, favourable and unfavourable happenings – all take on meaning through the *lwa,* leaving nothing to strike the faithful as absurd.

The hidden face of the universe

The superior and invisible spirits are born into the world. They may have been important people who made a mark on the history of their clan or tribe, ancestors whose memory endures among their descendants, animals or natural elements such as thunder or storms.

They all act as links between the visible and the invisible. They explain the origins of the world,

Tradition associates the deity Ibo Lélé – represented in the *vèvè* opposite by the jar marked with the conjoined V of fertility – with the glorious ancestor Dessalines (here, in a sheet-metal cutout).

It is claimed that Dessalines, warrior and founder of the independent state of Haiti in 1804, drew his courage from the power of voodoo. In some temples he is honoured as a native *lwa.*

The *lwa* reside mostly in trees, springs and rivers, to which their servants make numerous pilgrimages. Left, a ceremony around the mapou (silk-cotton) tree on the site of Nan Souvenance.

representing its hidden side, shadowed and deep: the very essence of life. All the *lwa* have a mythical story that, however, is tied to human history. Without losing their own identity, all have been connected with the Catholic saints, a telling sign not only of the conditions of their existence but also of their capacity

for transformation, adaptation and survival.

There are many *lwa* that intervene in the affairs of the living. This might lead one to consider voodoo a pantheistic religion, except that the *lwa* are not thought of as gods but as supernatural beings who serve as mediators between God and humans. As in many African regions, monotheism holds sway. While the Christian God was forcibly adopted by the followers of

Forbidden by the Church, voodoo made use of the rites and symbols of Catholicism to survive and develop. Behind every saint, faithfully taken from Catholic iconography, a *lwa* is celebrated. Above, Saint John the Baptist stands for Chango, the spirit of light and fire, and Saint Claire, with lowered eyes, is honoured as the mother of the *marassa* twins.

Most of the voodoo ceremonies unfold around a *poteau-mitan* (left), which the *lwa* use to come to earth.

voodoo, that being took on many of the traits of the African supreme being. Both distant and close at hand, s/he is too great to trouble her/himself with humans, instead delegating the task of organizing the world to the *lwa,* with whom humans can make agreements.

From Guinea to 'poteau-mitan': the *lwa* itinerary

The faithful believe that the *lwa* come from Africa, more specifically, a section of Africa confined to Guinea, irretrievably lost and considered purely mythical. According to the deported slaves, the *lwa* in their turn made the voyage out of Africa to the Caribbean. Before landing in Haiti, they took on certain practices pertaining to specific paths and places to gather. For example, the *lwa* from Guinea reunite on a sacred mountain, called Ville-au-Camps, in the northwest of the country. Before descending the mountain to return to the subterranean waters where they dwell, they trade experiences.

Even so, they do not disembark just anywhere or distribute themselves any which way. Their course is marked out, all the more rigorously as their mission is to structure the foundations of space for the living. In the centre of the voodoo temple, or *oufò,* is a peristyle, the space devoted to the ceremony in honour of the *lwa.* In the middle of the peristyle rises the *poteau-mitan,* the post that links the heavenly and earthly worlds. As such, it represents the royal path taken by the *lwa* to meet with humans. Offerings to the *lwa* and symbolic *vèvè* are placed around its

The *lwa* have always been at the heart of Haiti's political vicissitudes. They even become involved in disputes and control, and get rid of or help elect the presidents. Voodoo painters are fascinated with the influence of spiritual powers on the country's future. Cameau Rameau titled his canvas below *The Voodoo Gods Incline Towards the Fate of Haiti,* and in it he assembled the main

African *lwa,* or the Rada *lwa* – Azaka, Ezili Freda, Ogou, Ezili Dantò and Baron Samdi – to seek their counsel on the bloody dramas that surround the exercise of power in Haiti.

base. Attracted by these signals and rolls of the drum, the *lwa* arrive to dance in the bodies of the faithful. In Haitian voodoo, the *poteau-mitan* is painted with the two *lwa* Dambala and Ayida Wèdo, symbolized by two snakes, so that the pole resembles the tree of life, around which the voodoo dances whirl.

Rada, Kongo, Petro

Whether they originated as the protective spirits of clans or deified ancestors, the categories of *lwa* in Haiti reflect the various African ethnic groups. They are regrouped into families called nations, or *nanchon,* which are divided by different rituals. Each ritual has distinctive ceremonies, with its own greetings, cheers, dances, musical instruments and type of animal marked out for sacrifice.

There are three important rituals. The ritual known as Rada honours spirits from Dahomey, in principle considered the 'good *lwa*', called *lwa*

A gwé, the master of the sea, whose *vèvè* is being drawn above, is mostly served by fishermen and those who travel on the water. The Siren, *lwa* of springs and rivers, is considered his wife. The couple is depicted here in a sheet-metal cutout.

A mong the *lwa* honoured since the creation of voodoo in Saint-Domingue and invoked for initiation ceremonies and baptisms of drums are Dambala and Ayida Wèdo, symbolized by two snakes. Belonging to the Rada family, they are aquatic *lwa*, in contrast to the Petro *lwa*, who control the element of fire. In the same category is found Ezili, goddess of sensuality and love, whose *vèvè* is a heart. Three-horned Bosu (below), sometimes classified as Rada, sometimes as Petro, in Dahomey was a sacred monster whom the kings served.

from Guinea, or *lwa-Ginen*. All initiation ceremonies (through which the follower becomes *ounsi,* that is, the wife or husband of a *lwa*) always use the Rada ritual.

The Kongo ritual relates to the *lwa* of Bantu origin. They are less popular than the Rada spirits. They may be distinguished by the sacrifice of dogs, which they love to receive, as well as by their exuberance.

The *lwa* celebrated by the Petro ritual mostly come from the colony of Saint-Domingue itself. These are called the Creole *lwa*. Highly vengeful, they are considered 'bitter' as opposed to the Rada *lwa,* which are 'gentle'. They are used in the practice of magic. In the Petro ritual, certain Kongo *lwa* and even some of the Rada *lwa* appear, although taking on violent characteristics.

The classification of *lwa* by their rituals is not always firmly maintained. Some secondary rituals were introduced into the Rada, such as Nago, which calls up spirits from Yoruba, very early integrated into Dahomian voodoo. *Lwa* from Kongo sometimes join in the Petro.

Papa Legba, head of them all

Not every *lwa* carries the same weight or holds the same position in each of the pantheons corresponding to the three main rituals. To start with, one of the *lwa* is considered the head of all the others and for all the rituals: Legba. The first to be invoked during worship, he serves to open the gate that separates humans from the supernatural world, as his song explains:

Papa Legba ouvri bayè-a pou mwen
Pou mwen pase
Lè ma tounen, ma salyié lwa yo.
(Papa Legba, open the gate for me,
So I can go through,
When I return, I will pay honour to the *lwa*.)

Like Prometheus in Greek mythology, Legba stole God's secret and passed it on to humanity. He protects the entrance to temples and houses as well as crossroads, where he is known as *mèt-kalfou* (crossroads master). As noon and midnight approach, Legba turns into a spirit of magic. Both defensive and offensive magical practices are carried out under his auspices. In Cuba, he is called Ogu or Elegba; in Brazil, Eshu, where he is sometimes associated with the Christian devil, a coupling that does not seem to trouble the followers of Brazilian *candomblé*.

Ogou the Red and Baron Samdi

The other voodoo *lwa* that hierarchically rank below Legba rule various realms of nature and human activities.

Ogou Feray, *lwa* of blacksmiths, fire and war (his *vèvè* is shown above), has a sabre or the machete of the Yoruba tribe of Nigeria as his emblem. The *lwa* of the Ogou family (Ogou Badagri, Ogou Balendjo, and so on) participate in the Nago ritual. Their preferred animals are the ram and the red rooster.

A wily *lwa*, Legba is the master of crossroads, the guardian of the temple entrance and the indispensable intermediary between the deities and humans. In Haiti, Legba often shares the attributes of Saint Peter (opposite), who guards the keys to heaven, and sometimes of Saint Lazarus; as the latter, he appears as an old man leaning on a crutch, capable of angry attacks. Although he continues to represent danger and disorder, he has lost some of the phallic appearance he still retains in Benin (left).

Baron Samdi, head of the spirits of the dead called the Gédé, always wears black and a top hat. His lascivious dances, called *banda*, imitate sexual coupling. Under his auspices acts of magic and sorcery, called 'expeditions' after Saint Expedit, the Baron's Catholic counterpart, are carried out in cemeteries or at crossroads. In the representation of him by the painter Edouard Duval Carrié in 1991 (left), his uncanny resemblance to the former dictator François Duvalier and his exposed phallus with blood streaming out of it evoke the evil forces that have dominated Haitian political life.

Ogou, a *lwa* of the Nago family who is part of the Rada rite, is known for his warrior qualities. His favourite colour, red, refers as well to fire, which is his province. He is also the *lwa* of fertility, as he has intimate relations with many other *lwa*, including Ezili, who personifies beauty and sensuality and lives in the waters. Ogou is said to be the cousin of Azaka, the *lwa* of agriculture. His adopted son, the *lwa* Brave-Gédé, whose symbolic attribute is a phallus, presides over death.

In the same pantheon lives the Gédé family, with Baron Samdi at its head. The Gédé represent an ethnic group conquered by the royal family of

Abomey, many of whom were shipped to Saint-Domingue as slaves. Having disappeared in Benin, in Haiti they became the *lwa* of death. The Gédé dances take place in both town and country during the month of November, particularly the first two days of the month, considered almost a national holiday. The Gédé *lwa*, with their attributes of death – the colour black, nasal voice, undertaker's appearance, cotton plugs in the nostrils – provoke fear, although their dances, songs and obscene talk inspire merriment.

A demanding helper

The *lwa* ensure continuity between the living and the dead, as well as the stability and durability of the family.

Ogou Batala, Ogou Feray, *lwa* of fire and of war, belong to the Nago family, which had already been integrated into voodoo worship in Dahomey. Ogou takes his image from the Catholic Saint James the Greater, the vanquisher of the Moors, always depicted on the attack, his sword drawn, on a white horse (above). When his servants are possessed by him, they put on red neckerchiefs, carry swords and flail energetically, even brutally. Ogou likes to receive as an offering a red cock, sometimes a bull, like the one shown on the left, which is painted on the wall of a peristyle and dedicated to Ogou.

The duality of the icons

The figures of Catholic saints that decorate the walls of voodoo temples are evocations of the *lwa*. Opposite, the Mater Dolorosa is Ezili Freda. Above left, Saint Joseph evokes Loko, the healing *lwa*, a herb doctor. Saint Patrick chasing away the snakes of Ireland (above) stands for Dambala Wèdo because of the snake imagery. Saint John the Baptist, shown on the left with his sheep, is allied with Chango, *lwa* of luck.

The angel, the pipe and the sack

Saint Isidore is the patron of farmers. In the voodoo pantheon, he is transformed into Cousin Azaka with the same role, shown in the mural opposite by the angel driving a plough pulled by two oxen. In the centre of his *vèvè* a cock, a sheep's head and a bottle containing spirits are placed as offerings. All the *lwa* of the Azaka family are related to agricultural work. Like them, and like the peasants, Cousin Azaka (left) smokes a clay pipe, wears blue clothing and a red kerchief, and, above all, carries the characteristic *macoute* (sack) of woven straw used by peasants in the fields.

Cousin Azaka bears no resemblance whatsoever to Ezili (pictured on p. 76). A mulatto with long hair, always adorned with jewelry, Ezili Fred is known for her scandalous life: mistress of Agwé, *lwa* of the sea, she is also Dambala's concubine, carries on an affair with Ogou, and is courted by the *lwa* Gédé Nibo. Sometimes jealous and sometimes melancholy, she is prone to violent fits of anger.

They hold responsibility for fertility and health and the attainment of material and spiritual wealth. In general, people inherit *lwa* from the family; tied to a piece of earth, they are passed on along with the land from parents to children. It also happens that *lwa* announce themselves in dreams, hardly leaving the individuals so favoured any choice; if refused, the *lwa* might persecute them, sending them sickness or various other misfortunes.

In the voodoo pantheon, the *lwa* are sometimes bad and sometimes good; a fixed dualism does not apply. In Haiti, one hears often of completely evil spirits – cannibalistic *lwa* who might devour their followers or carry out reprisals against neglectful worshippers. Many Petro and Kongo *lwa,* for example, are considered dangerous, but if they are properly ministered to, they grant as many boons as *lwa* of other families. Thus, in certain parts of the country where the *lwa* are called *diab,* or devils, it means only that the voodoo followers have

The *lwa* are known to punish negligent or careless servants. They carry out an arrest, called *sep*: they take over the offenders' bodies with brutality, throwing them to the ground and making them crawl with crossed feet until they take refuge in the cavity carved out for the *lwa* in the courtyard of the *oufò* (above).

The voodoo worshipper does not consider the devil as the incarnation of absolute evil. Certainly he is a negative force, but one open to neg-otiation. In addition, the *lwa* are called indiscrim-inately *zanj* (angels), saints, mysteries or *diab* (devils).

absorbed the Christian vocabulary, without for a moment believing in the Christian devil. There is even a Petro *lwa* known as Lucifer.

One can never be too careful

As in many other religious systems, unlimited power is often ascribed to the *lwa,* making them fill all manner of functions to the point that they take over the individual's entire life or seem to become the reason for all the follower's misfortunes. Such a bond can be broken by going to a voodoo priest, who interprets the messages and qualities of the *lwa*. The power of a *lwa* can always be counterbalanced by that of another or mastered by a specific ritual known to the voodoo priest.

While the practice of magic and sorcery is generally disapproved of by the voodoo faithful, they are aware

A *manbo* (above) and an *oungan* (left) prepare to consult the *lwa.* On each one's altar (*pé*) rests a jumble of bottles, jugs, dishes, necklaces, sacred stones, candles, emblems of the *lwa* and various ingredients used in the concoction of potions and magic charms to protect their clients. The *oungan* proudly displays his *asson,* covered with a network of snake vertebrae. Traditional emblem of the voodoo priest's power, it recalls the spiritual powers of Guinea, where Dan, the snake god, was worshipped by the royal family of Dahomey.

Saints Cosmas and Damian (left) are identified with the twin *lwa* called the *lwa marassa*. This category of *lwa* appears in all the rites (Rada, Nago, Petro, Kongo and Creole). They are thought to be gifted with extraordinary powers, including making the rain fall and providing remedies to the sick. Playing an elevated role in the voodoo pantheon, they are generally invoked at the beginning of ceremonies, just after Legba. Their duality coincides with the androgynous double god Mawu-Lisa and with the Yoruba gods Obatala and Odudua, which symbolize primeval harmony, and the original union of sky and earth and of day and night. On the other hand, the *marassa* are also jealous and vindictive. Twin children in a family, living or dead, are deified, and they are given a ceremony in their honour punctually every year, on 4 January, Easter eve or Christmas; failure to do so is certain to bring misfortune.

that dangerous forces cling to the edges of the voodoo system, ready to spring into action. Thus they will make arrangements to guard against bad fortune and take protective measures with analogous weapons. For that purpose, another category of *lwa* exists, called *lwa-achté*, which can be purchased from the *oungan*. They hold out the promise of more effective help than that offered by the family *lwa*. Purchasing *lwa* carries a certain risk, for their protection may come at a high price. If purchasers fail to meet their obligations, the *lwa-achté* will fly into a terrible rage and heap calamities on their owners' families.

Twins and ancestors

On top of all that, the voodoo faithful are subject not only to single *lwa* but also to twin or *lwa marassa*, thought to be more powerful than ordinary *lwa* by virtue of the union they symbolize. All of the rituals include them. They have the peculiarity of being extremely fussy about the services they demand. The least negligence shown by their relatives brings retaliation. They regularly require offerings, called *mangé-marassa* – a sacrificial meal consisting of baby goat or chicken – to be served in special dishes made from two or three calabash bowls bound together, or else left in three holes scooped out in the courtyard of the house or voodoo temple. When the *marassa* have been satisfied, they provide recipes for medicines made from plants or herbs.

Family ancestors, who have turned into something approaching spirits, are the subject of a periodic worship whose effectiveness is sworn by. It seems that the recently deceased can more rapidly grasp the problems of those they left behind. In this respect, the cult of the dead is basic to the schema of voodoo beliefs, as it is directly through them that the faithful are supposed to attract the favours of the *lwa*, or at least find a place in their symbolic chain.

The twin *lwa* may number two, three or four, depending on how many babies are born at once. The first two are called *marassa*; any that follow are called *marassa dosu* (boy) or *dosa* (girl). In the middle of the *vèvè* that represents them (above) are two eggs that symbolize fertility; the conjoined Vs on the right and left stand for the *marassa dosu* and *dosa*, signs of primeval androgyny. During ceremonies in the twins' honour, the offerings are served in buckets and clay pitchers, carried in a unique holder (left).

Unbearable if regarded solely as a brutal penalty exacted by nature, death instead may become a source of regeneration for society when it is mediated by means of specific rites. Through them, the living furnish the dead with strength, thus helping to propel them through the waters towards the home of the voodoo spirits.

CHAPTER 5

THE CULT OF THE DEAD

One of the places to go in order to talk with the dead, get complaints off one's chest, seek comfort in moments of distress: the cemetery of Port-au-Prince (opposite). The voodoo worshipper believes that cemeteries are under the control of the cross of Baron Samdi (right), the leader of the spirits of the dead.

During the slave period, missionaries had been struck by the amount of energy the slaves invested in the Catholic rites of death, to the point that they somehow succeeded in taking over the ritual. The slaves managed this despite the tendency of slave owners to give their dead slaves only the most perfunctory of funerary rites. Ever since the abolition of slavery, the mass for the dead has remained the major contribution of the Catholic Church to the voodoo follower. More important than baptism, Communion or the worship of saints, the mass for the dead is viewed by the faithful not as a means of winning God's favour on behalf of the deceased but as a fully integrated voodoo rite, expressing a desire for social acknowledgment. Since it reaches to some extent into every level of society, the church is ideally suited to function as a special gathering place for this rite.

Caring for the dead so the living may rest in peace

Whenever a death is acknowledged by society, it brings social acknowledgment to the living. The cult of the dead practised by slaves recognized that their ties with the dead shaped their social mores and behaviour. Thus it is not fear of death that drives what looks like a passion for the dead in the voodoo religion but the followers' desire to recover and assert their human dignity. To this end they will use whatever means they have available, including Catholic ceremonies, to pay respects to their dead. In the outlook of voodoo, death is an event that strikes foremost at the social fabric, that is, the family and community, rather than the deceased individual.

The spirits of the dead, called Gédé, are represented by a symbolic drawing (left). The cross signifies the crossing of roads, not the cross of Christ, and it carries on its vertical post the V symbols that indicate the androgynous nature of the Gédé. At the bottom right is their masculine emblem.

The rites consist almost entirely of the effort to make the death real and lasting, so the dead will not haunt the living and make their lives miserable. Death is not treated as a permanent source of anguish; people do not face its reality without the support of the social group or the community.

Of course, in contemporary life traditional patterns of behaviour tend to vanish, especially as people move from rural to urban areas and from lower to middle and upper classes, which are more affected by modernization.

In the countryside, taking the dead to the cemetery calls for precautions. Those carrying the coffin must pretend to lose their way in order to confuse the dead so they cannot possibly find the road that leads back to the house. Above, a burial in the country.

A house 'in mourning' receives visits from neighbours (left). Sometimes the house in which an inhabitant has died will display purple curtains, purple being the symbolic colour of mourning, placed in the entry doors. Everything must be done to create around the death an event that brings together the community. In the house, a room where the deceased is laid out is reserved for visitors (opposite). Preparing the deceased for burial falls to a specialist in sacred rites, such as the *oungan* below.

Avoiding contamination

When someone dies, one of the family members present gives a cry, called a *rèl,* that announces the death to the neighbourhood. Friends and relatives soon gather. A campaign begins to get rid of everything reminiscent of the deceased, starting with his or her clothes and goods. In other words, the person's dying becomes, little by little, a production engaged in by the entire community. Its object is to separate the dead from the living, to draw a boundary between the former and the community he or she comes from; this cannot be accomplished in a single day.

First of all, since death is the separation from the body of the various spiritual elements that together make up a human being, it is essential to watch and make sure that all the elements disperse as they should and find new places to go. During the first few moments of death, the deceased's soul lingers near the body, even moving about the house. It becomes a danger for the living, as it can contaminate them with death by dragging them into it. All the preparations and careful procedures surrounding the funeral rites are focused on organizing the definitive departure of the dead. When this is accomplished, the process

‘ Even the most destitute family does not hesitate to sacrifice its last pennies to ensure a proper funeral for one of its members. In such spending…there may be an element of vanity and concern for "what the neighbours might say", yet this ostentation has a deeper cause.’

Alfred Métraux

that reintegrates the dead into the community, as the 'potential protector', can be begun.

The spirits break away

Before the funeral rites can take place, the deceased voodoo follower has to be subjected to the ritual called *dessounen,* which disengages the protective spirit, or *lwa-mèt-tèt,* to which the dead person had been dedicated. Until this rite is performed, the dead person is considered still alive. The voodoo priest begins by placing friends and relatives some distance away. Then he takes up the *asson,* a rattle that symbolizes his power over the spirits, and calls the *lwa-mèt-tèt,* residing still in the head of the deceased. When the head is seen to make a movement, it means the *lwa* has left the body. Sometimes it goes to a family member in the house, who becomes the heir of that *lwa.* The deceased's soul now can be put in a pot – that is, a sample of locks of hair and

nail clippings are placed in the pot, which puts a stop to the use of the dead person's soul for any evil purpose.

These practices and beliefs explain why the person, usually a woman, who bathes the body holds

conversations with the deceased while carrying out her job. The deceased leaves for the invisible world loaded with messages that he or she will remember at the end of the journey.

The tradition of addressing the deceased, very common in black Africa, has been preserved in Haiti, for the vigil over the dead as well as for the bathing ritual.

The ties of community grow tighter

Relatives, friends and neighbours gather for the night and remain until dawn. Card tables are set up for the men; women make tea and coffee. The gathering is punctuated by sobs and wails, by reproaches and requests addressed to the deceased, by prayers and hymns.

However, the vigil functions largely as a communal diversion. The participants

Homage to the dead needs to be periodically reaffirmed. All the members of a family, even the most distant, come together for a service dedicated to talking with the dead and seeking their advice in, for example, cases of disputes over inheritance. Surrounding a *pé-savann* (a former priest's assistant who is versed in the prayers and hymns of the Catholic ceremonies) and dressed in white are the relatives of the deceased (opposite above). A goat with a white kerchief tied around its head looks over the delicacies offered to the dead (rum, sparkling drinks, melon, corn, peas and so on), which almost duplicate those of the death watch. On a table in the living room more food and drink is displayed. One of the significant moments of the 'service' is when the goat – which will later be sacrificed – darts into the living room and clambers on to the table to taste the various dishes (opposite below). This indicates that the ceremony is successful. After this moment, the dead are believed to be pleased with their ceremony, and the dances begin to the sound of the drum (above left).

recount the life of the deceased and share anecdotes, stories and riddles to lighten the mood.

The success of the vigil certainly reflects the dead person's social prominence. More important, however, is its goal to overcome despair in the face of the irrevocability of death by outbidding it with an affirmation of life.

If the family of the deceased is poor or lives in the country, the coffin is supported on the heads of a single row of bearers, often only two men. On the way to the cemetery, family

The many precautions taken around the deathbed reveal that the retirement from the world of the living needs to be well organized and represents a long, complex and dangerous process. The washing and dressing of the dead, the placement in the coffin, the trip from house to church and then cemetery must follow very strict guidelines to prevent the dead from getting back home, so that he or she cannot return to trouble the living. The burial is only one more stage in the production of the definitive departure.

members cry out and fall to the ground, as if the deceased gripped them in the manner of a voodoo spirit. Signs of sincere grief must be clearly presented on the grave (opposite above, a typical crown for a tomb) so that the deceased will in return bring the family benefits.

The period of mourning serves to bring the living into empathy with the dead so that the latter's invisible status can be confirmed. It may last from six months to two years, according to the mourner's degree of closeness to the dead. The lifting of the period of mourning indicates that the deceased has finally retreated from the world of the living.

The family must stay in the cemetery and keep the deceased company to the last moment (below), so that he or she will be successful in the long voyage ahead into the world of the dead. Voodoo followers do not have the option of not honouring their dead, for the latter would come to pester them in dreams or torment them with illness or setbacks.

'Manjé-lèmò': provisions

Once the separation rites have been accomplished, family members and friends periodically offer meals to the dead, called *manjé-lèmò,* believing that the dead need food and drink while undergoing the journey in the invisible world beneath the waters. Even before that, the dead feel cold and must be warmed, by means of the rite called *boule-zen.* The pots, or *po-tèt,* that hold the locks of hair and nail clippings symbolizing the deceased's soul are passed through fire. Pots or pans are filled up with oil and a fire is lighted, signifying the departure of the spirit of the dead towards the waters where they live.

Once again, the deceased is subjected to questioning. From this moment on, he or she has the ability to grant the requests made by the living. Holding a dialogue with the dead, the living

also hope to discover the secrets of life and death newly available to the dead. As the dead are nourished, their forces flow back to the living. Since the dead are close to the voodoo spirits, themselves being nominal spirits, the well-fed dead can give advice in dreams, confer gifts, transmit knowledge about plants and leaves with medicinal properties, even foretell a winning lottery or *borlette* (a popular game of chance) number – in short, hand out all kinds of favours and riches.

The Gédé, phallic and facetious *lwa* of death

One of the most important of the voodoo celebrations is the ceremony in honour of the *lwa* of the dead, or the *lwa* Gédé, which in most *oufò*, or voodoo temples, occurs on 1 and 2 November. All the public cemeteries, as

well as private ones on family property in the country, are visited. People pull weeds around the tombs, which have been whitened for the occasion. During this period, in the markets or on the streets, one might come upon people possessed by the Gédé: for the space of the holiday, these *lwa* take over, and it is imprudent to refuse their attentions. On the day of the dead, however, the appearance of the Gédé provokes laughter, for they are

The *lwa* of the dead represent an imposing family and appear in all voodoo rites. They form what is called an 'escort' and go by different names depending on the role they play. For example, there is Gédé Nibo, assistant gravedigger, who shows up, according to a well-known song, as 'a handsome youth, dressed all in white like a deputy learning to climb the steps of the national palace'; Gédé Fouillé, who digs the graves; Gédé Loraj, who presides over those who died violently, by gunshot.

Showing his attachment to the Gédé, this *oungan*, who lives near a cemetery, wears sunglasses and smokes a cigar while waiting for clients. Here he demonstrates the sometimes acrobatic and often sexual positions taken during a possession. With his sunglasses removed, the possessed *oungan* adopts the blank stare of a cadaver or the haggard expression of a madman.

phallic *lwa* who tell dirty stories, perform lascivious and obscene dances and spend their time playing jokes on the voodoo faithful, such as stealing their money or personal property. They also like to eat well and drink rum. Some *oufò* display on the altar a huge wooden phallus which is offered to the 'possessed' as they fall into their trance. The eccentric behaviour of the Gédé actually expresses the art of turning death into satire. Playing death in order to outwit it – this may be their scheme, for if death is unavoidable, outplaying it with life lets one face it successfully. The anthropologist Alfred Métraux wrote, 'Their entry onto the peristyle stage is always greeted with joy by all present. Everyone knows they can be relied on to introduce a vein of frank gaiety into the most serious ceremonies. Their habit of talking through their noses is by itself comic enough....'

Baron Samdi, also called Baron Cimetière or Baron La Croix, is the leader of the Gédé. People appeal to him most often concerning the problems of daily life. The following pages show two altars dedicated to the Baron: always a cross, one or more skulls, a hat, glasses, bottles of rum given in offering, candles and so on. These are generally places where magic and sorcery are carried on.

The *lwa* are dedicated to serving humans, but they will not bestow their largesse until they are welcomed and well fed. A very specific protocol must be followed before they appear. Possession, initiation and mystical marriage are special forms of close contact with the *lwa*. Only by achieving closeness with the *lwa* can humans learn their fate, although they are powerless to change it.

CHAPTER 6
'MANJÉ-LWA', 'DANSÉ-LWA': THE SERVICES

Huts, called *kay-mistè*, are built to receive the *lwa* and filled with their objects or symbols. Opposite, the attributes of Cousin Azaka, *lwa* of agriculture: the *macoute*, the cane and the straw hat of a peasant. For protection one can buy acts of magic; ingredients, such as skulls and ropes (right) are always at hand.

The voodoo religion works on two different levels: the individual and the community. All followers have at their command a *lwa-rasin,* or a *lwa* inherited from their parents; they often place in their bedrooms a

At Easter, ceremonies are held in the *lakou* of Nan Souvenance under the mapou trees.

small *rogatoire,* or altar, on which they place a candle to call up their *lwa* and a picture or image of the corresponding Catholic saint. For the celebration of the family *lwa* or those acquired by initiation, the faithful are joined to the confraternity comprised of members of the same *oufò.*

Secrecy in the country and caution in the outskirts of town

Voodoo temples undoubtedly were built during the slave era, but only in the inaccessible reaches of the Maroon encampments. These sites saw the historic first experiments with the *lakou,* or compound. In large courtyards or settlements, many families lived together under the authority of a patriarch who also served as the religious leader. One of the huts was reserved for the worship of the *lwa,* the space's true owners. As soon as independence was declared in 1804, the former slaves eagerly built temples all over the country. However, as voodoo was not recognized officially, these centres of worship had to be placed either in the country, where they are still found, or on the outskirts of the capital and towns.

The 'oufò': the protocol for welcoming the voodoo spirits

The *oufò* is the temple where the *lwa,* here named 'the mysteries', have their own huts, *kay-mistè,* or huts of the mysteries, at their disposal and receive tribute from their servants. In the middle of the peristyle, where the dances take place and the *lwa* show themselves, various

An integral aspect of voodoo is the connection between the individual and the *lwa* he or she worships at home, in front of a *rogatoire* – a home altar – like the one pictured above, which has a chromolithograph of the Virgin (or the *lwa* Ezili), a sacred stone, and offerings of food and drink. In the *oufò,* each priest establishes a protocol for greeting the *lwa.* The altar, or *pé,* shown below is set with Baron Samdi's cross.

offerings of food or drink are placed around the base of the *poteau-mitan*. On the altar, or *pedji,* are arranged emblematic objects of the *lwa,* jugs swathed in their colours, bottles and *po-tèt* enclosing the souls of believers, all kept near the *lwa* to ensure their protection.

Three sacred drums of different sizes sit in the peristyle. Each *lwa* family has its own drums and rhythms, as the *lwa* appear only in response to their call. The *lwa* come to humans in dance. Some *oufò* are dedicated to the *lwa-Ginen,* or the *lwa* of Guinea, known for their goodness and gentleness, others to the Petro or Kongo, known for their aggressiveness. There exist *oufò* with two peristyles, one consecrated to the gentle *lwa,* the other, in the rear, to the bitter *lwa,* the ones to call on for help in the practice of offensive and defensive magic.

The altar of a voodoo temple (above) is often loaded with a variety of objects, which gives it an ornate and baroque character. Everything has a meaning and a purpose: bound-up magic packets called *wanga*; bottles of rum; attributes or emblems of the *lwa,* such as the horns of Ogou; images of the Virgin-Ezili; crosses of the Gédé; and dolls dedicated to Grann Brigitte, the wife of Baron Samdi. Other objects that might go on the altar are *govi,* or jugs, draped with necklaces indicating spiritual powers or dressed in the colours of the *lwa* (left).

Interpreter of the *lwa* among people, ambassador of humans to the *lwa*

The voodoo priest enjoys absolute power in his or her temple. Called *oungan* or *manbo* (female), or sometimes *bòkò* (implying a connection to sorcery), priests interpret the *lwa* language, act as psychological counsellors and practise medicine. Their power is believed to have been passed on through the family, by means of a dream, or by an illness that indicates their vocation. Their professional attribute, the *asson*, a kind of rattle made from a calabash, contains various elements, such as snake vertebrae, necklace beads and grains, and helps them direct the different stages of rituals.

The process of becoming a priest calls for a special initiation ceremony, carried out in secret after nine days of confinement. Before this, candidates have to undergo a period of habituation to life in the *oufò*. They are installed with a rite called *haussement,* or lifting, in which they are lifted by

The voodoo priest or priestess is usually feared and respected. Priests do not earn the symbol of their power, the *asson*, until they have undergone the trials of initiation, sometimes a long and always a dangerous process. Different ranks exist, such as *kanzo*, attained after completing a *boulé-zen* (burn-zinc), which consists of plunging one's left hand in a pot of boiling water in order to warm up the *lwa*.

others three times in the armchair consecrated to the priest. They then swear an oath to respect the powers of the *lwa*.

One hand for worship, the other for magic

The priest might cultivate relations with other priests who are better known or better qualified. To ensure that they are treated respectfully in the local area, they always ally themselves with the head of the rural section, the person who combines administrative, judicial and police powers for the country people, as well as with the local notables and politicians.

It is hard to keep tabs on the priests. It is believed that the *lwa* will sooner or later turn against *oungan* who are charlatans or who overstep their authority. There exists, however, a category of *oungan* who 'serve with both hands' – that is, magicians. They are considered to be in collusion with sorcerers.

A typical priest deals with the good *lwa*, or *lwa-Ginen*. He or she is often referred to as a doctor, although the *doktè-fey*, or leaf-doctors, claim a specialized knowledge of medicinal herbs and plants that they received as a special gift from the *lwa*. The priests treat only those illnesses with a supernatural cause. These treatments take place in the *oufò*, which can function as a clinic. They also hold consultations for a great number of people who come to seek advice, to have their dreams or misfortunes interpreted, or to ask for recipes (charms, magic potions, and so on) to find a lover, keep a woman, make a marriage happen, or succeed in business matters.

The 'oufò' society

Just as in a Catholic parish, the *oufò* has a regular vestry to ensure its success. Each *oufò* is served by a society that is virtually autonomous, although competition exists among individual *oungan*, some held in higher

The *lwa* can be capricious, and their demands sometimes need interpretation. As the *oungan* know the ways of the *lwa*, they are thought to have extraordinary powers. It is the rare servant of the *lwa* who has not availed him- or

herself of the *oungan*'s assistance. A voodoo follower in difficulties or suffering inexplicable woes calls on the *oungan*. He often crowds his altar with a cross, bound-up charms and various utensils that display his authority over the *lwa*. Here, one also finds a profusion of skulls, mirrors, candles, ropes, dolls and objects hung upside down.

esteem than others because they are considered to offer superior protection to their followers. Each society is governed by a hierarchy.

A ring of worshippers dressed in white forms around the *poteau-mitan.* These are the *ounsi,* or initiates, charged with singing and dancing. They whirl in the peristyle under the direction of the *ongenikòn,* or 'queen-

A voodoo ceremony unfolds somewhat like a play in which the spectators are also the actors. Seated on a special armchair in the peristyle, the *oungan* or *manbo* directs its progress. He or

singer'. Other roles filled by the society include the *laplas,* or master of ceremonies, the *bête-charge* (animal custodian), the administrator of the *oufò,* and the *pitit-fèy,* or diligent servant. All these roles give the organization the scope of a 'society'. Its members display strong solidarity, and when illness strikes it becomes a great source of mutual assistance. The *oungan,* the religious leader, is expected to offer help to the initiates who fill the various offices of his *oufò.*

A screen of Christian holidays

Voodoo ritual is rich, varied and complex. No ceremony completely resembles another one of its kind. Each priest has his or her favourite rites, secrets and special features to attract followers.

she begins with a litany of saints, prayers and hymns from the Catholic religion, all the while shaking the *asson,* then proceeds directly to the invocation of the *lwa* – starting with Legba – and then to the rite of *jété-dlo,* which consists of sprinkling water around the *poteau-mitan* towards the four points. The orchestra gradually joins in; the first drumrolls introduce the ritual sequences; and finally, the initiates dance.

Starting with Mardi Gras, and each weekend during the period of Lent, groups stroll through the countryside and the outskirts of towns, singing and dancing to the sound of bamboo trumpets called *vaccine*. These groups form the bands of *rara*. Each is led by a *mèt-rara*, usually an *oungan*. He directs the musicians and their instruments: the *vaccine*, the drums, the *konè* (a horn made of a long tube of rolled sheet metal), the *lambi* (a seashell that serves as a horn). They are accompanied by a chorus, dancers, acrobats and jugglers, all dressed in dazzling colours. The *major-jonc*, whose job is to attract the attention of the public, goes at the head of the procession and twirls a decorated cane (*jonc*), which he sometimes catches between his teeth. The sexual innuendos of the *rara* songs and dances recall the manners of the Gédé *lwa*. A band's outings, often organized from an *oufò*, are preceded by voodoo rituals, so that the band will know what road to take and will be protected from any evil spirits that they may come upon, especially at crossroads. The phenomenon of the *rara*, which began in the countryside, has lately made an appearance in urban centres.

Voodoo ceremonies are referred to as 'services'. They take place to mark annual holidays that are held in the *oufò,* to satisfy the special demand of a *lwa* servant, or at the behest of a family that pays all the expenses.

The voodoo liturgical calendar seems to follow closely that of the Catholic Church. The night of the *bains de chance,* or luck baths, often falls on Christmas. On 6 January (Epiphany), celebrated like New Year's Day by the voodoo followers, entire families gather around the *oufò*. All Saints' Day, 1 November, is the feast of the *lwa* of the dead, the Gédé. Lent is reserved for sorties by gangs of *rara*, groups connected with the *oufò*, which make the rounds of the streets and dance to a bamboo trumpet called a *vaccine*. Many Catholic patron saints' days are significant voodoo holidays as well: 16 July, the day dedicated to Our Lady of Mount Carmel (the Virgin

Mary), is called the Feast of Saut-d'Eau, consecrated to the *lwa* Ezili; 25 July, the feast of Saint James at Plaine-du-Nord, is that of Ogou; 26 July, assigned to Saint Anne, corresponds to the mother of Ezili; and so on.

The reception of the *lwa*

A typical voodoo ceremony has two main parts. First come the rites of entry: a parade of the *oufò*'s flags; greetings to the sacred objects, including the drums;

One of the requirements of serving the *lwa* well is offering them sacrifices, because they only feel strong enough to give their protection when they are well fed. Left, a *manbo* prepares a bull to be sacrificed in honour of Ogou. Sometimes Ogou is offered a cock (below), here turned towards the four cardinal points before being killed.

the rites of orientation of the sacred objects towards the four cardinal points to define the sacred space; and finally the invocations of the different *lwa*, preceded by long Catholic prayers and the litanies of the saints. The air gradually warms from the dancing of the initiated to the rhythms of the drum around the *poteau-mitan*.

The *lwa* who participate in the ceremony need to eat to recover their strength, the better to grant favours to their servants. The second part of the ceremony features the sacrifice, known as the *manjé-lwa*.

The ceremony is often directed by one or many worshippers who get together to buy the animals – goat, sheep, bull or chicken – preferred by the *lwa* from whom special favours are desired. Prepared dishes, such as grilled corn and cake, and spirits are left on the foot of the *poteau-mitan,* along with animals adorned with the colours of the *lwa* to which they are being sacrificed.

The sacrifice

The person who has offered the service, or the *commanditaire,* whose head is wrapped in a red kerchief, samples the foods placed before the animal, which becomes the substitute victim for the *lwa*. The animal is offered the foods prepared for it; if it eats them, it indicates that the *lwa* have accepted the sacrifice. The animal then undergoes a special preparation, known as

The *lwa* enter the bodies of the faithful during the songs and dances performed in their honour. In this respect, the drums play a central role, creating rhythms that bring the heartbeats of the faithful and the *lwa* together. Above, the drums of the Rada rite. They are usually three in number: the *manman tambour,* or principal drum; the second; and the *boula,* the smallest. Certain drums are dedicated to the African Guinea *lwa*, like the *asòtò* (left). This drum is treated almost as an idol, being made from a 'wood which has much blood'.

its 'toilette': its head, neck and feet are washed with an infusion made with leaves, and it is perfumed.

The sacrificer must be someone who belongs to the *oufò*. Before carrying out the office, he or she has taken purifying baths. After killing the animal, he or she drinks a few drops of its blood, then heaves the body on to his back. The faithful come to rub against it or use its blood to draw a cross on their foreheads. The animal is then directed towards the four points of the compass, presenting it to the supernatural powers of the four 'sides'. It is carved and cooked outside the peristyle, in the courtyard of the *oufò*.

'Dansé-lwa': the fit of possession

The crucial part of the ceremony is the manifestation of the *lwa*. After the *oungan* draws the *vèvè* on the ground, a drawing symbolic of the *lwa* whose design was arrived at in the course of the session, and the beating of the drums and special songs reach them, the *lwa* arrive.

The faithful who have been entered by the *lwa* are seized by a 'fit of possession'. Appearing drunken, they sketch gestures reminiscent of the *lwa* who have selected them for their 'horses'. It is said that the *lwa* 'mount' their servants, using their bodies as instruments of self-expression. Thus, the latter take the form of the *lwa*: those possessed by Ogou will display a sabre, by Azaka a pipe and a peasant's satchel. They dance in the steps specific to their *lwa*. Those possessed by Dambala throw themselves to the ground in convulsions and crawl, darting their tongues, like snakes.

No one present seems surprised by the appearance of the *lwa*. The spirits dance in their servants' heads, sing, convey their greetings, talk, and perhaps announce good or bad happenings. Once awakened, the possessed person remembers nothing of the event.

Orchestration

Sometimes onlookers fall into trances as well. The same *lwa* can 'ride' many people at once during a ceremony.

The *lwa* cannot enter their servants' bodies without first being received by ritual salutations. The onset of the trance is hazardous, as the *lwa* seizes his 'horse' wildly; the *oungan* or *manbo* must spin the possessed person (above, the twirling movement that the priest has the servant make). In every case, the initiates pay close attention to anyone about to 'fall into a trance' (opposite below, initiates take charge of one of their number 'in a fit'). Once the *lwa* has been well received by his 'horse' and the other servants, the dance goes on, expressing the satisfaction of the *lwa* at the welcome they have received.

It always happens that, depending on the rhythm of the drum, other *lwa* join in, the fit of possession being contagious in nature. The *lwa* sample the dishes prepared for them in the peristyle and help themselves to pieces of the animal sacrificed to them, which have been

• The explanation of mystic trance given by disciples of Voodoo is simple. A *loa* moves into the head of an individual having first driven out "the good big angel" (*gros bon ange*) – one of the two souls that everyone carries in himself. This eviction of the soul is responsible for the tremblings and convulsions which characterize the opening stages of trance. Once the good angel has gone the person possessed experiences a feeling of total emptiness as though he were fainting. His head whirls, the calves of his legs tremble.... From now on it is the god's personality and not his own which is expressed in his bearing and words.... The relationship between the *loa* and the man seized is compared to that which joins a rider to his horse. •

Alfred Métraux
Voodoo in Haiti, 1972

Those who seek a fixed personal bond with a *lwa* undergo initiation, which includes certain trials, beginning with confinement in an *oufò*. Initiation is like a rebirth, one must die first before achieving it.

placed in holes dug out in the courtyard.

Nothing is left to chance in a voodoo ceremony, even if it gives way to all-out revelling. The *oungan* or *manbo* makes arrangements to watch over and regulate the comings and goings of the *lwa* in the bodies of the faithful. *Lwa* who make unscheduled appearances in the head of a dancer are promptly sent away. One of the functions of the priest consists of knowing how to restrain or laugh with a *lwa*, according to the voodoo expression. Perfectly schooled in the habits and behaviour of the *lwa*, he or she communicates with them through gestures that tell them to continue to show themselves or leave.

The appearance of the *lwa* is the hallmark of a successful ceremony. Without their protection, individuals are cast adrift and become the toys or targets of all the unknown spiritual powers (souls of the dead, unregulated evil spirits) that their enemies could muster against them.

'Die to be reborn': the initiation

For this reason, a servant of the *lwa* agrees to the initiation, whose main object is to establish the *lwa* in the head once and for all. This is called the *lwa-mèt-tèt*, entrusted with directing and protecting his charge as long as he or she lives. The decision to become an *ounsi*, or initiate, might come through a dream, an illness or an inheritance.

The ritual of initiation lasts a week, sometimes a fortnight, but it has lost the complexity that it still retains in Africa. The neophyte, or *ougno,* is first confined in an *oufò* under the guidance of a sponsor who will help him or her through the difficult time. The neophyte gradually learns all about the *lwa* to whom he or she will be devoted, as well as plants and leaves with curative powers. Also learned is how to become a 'mystic', that is, one who seeks to deepen one's rapport with the spirits.

The ceremony that concludes the ritual of initiation is the exit of the novices. Dressed in white, a white kerchief knotted around the head, which has been covered for the duration of the confinement with a poultice made of medicinal herbs and foods, such as grilled corn and rice, the novices emerge in a procession and take their places in the peristyle. If they are possessed by the *lwa-mèt-tèt* during the ceremony, it is a clear sign that the *lwa* are now tied to the lives of their servants until death, which will give rise to the rite called *dessounen,* the retirement of the *lwa* attached to the initiate.

A special *lwa* is reserved for initiation – Ayizan, whose *vèvè,* or symbolic drawing (left), basically consists of the two conjoined Vs of primeval androgyny. The central part represents leaves of the royal palm. Ayizan bestows on initiates knowledge of herbs and plants that provide cures or protection. The wife of Legba, she symbolizes authority and power. Branches of the royal palm are usually suspended on the posts of the *oufò* to protect them and hold evil spirits at bay.

After the confinement, the trials of initiation continue with the *lavé-têt* (the washing of the head with infusions of herbs and medicinal plants) and a strict diet of, for example, boiled corn without salt. Through these trials, the initiates earn different degrees of mystical powers. Opposite, a *manbo* holds the *asson* in her right hand.

Contracting a 'mystical marriage' with a *lwa* confers benefits, but the new spouse must fulfil the demands to prove fidelity. The first task is to furnish the hut where he or she will be received. Left, a bridal chamber for Ezili.

An additional precaution: the mystical marriage

The decision to make a mystical marriage could be arrived at voluntarily by the voodoo follower, who in difficult situations might wish to be assured of having the *lwa*'s aid at hand. It could also be the *lwa*'s choice, who through various means, including spontaneous possessions, signals a desire to be joined in marriage. The ceremony resembles a proper Catholic marriage, but it is presided over by a *pè-savann,* or 'bush priest'. This former beadle or sexton, having attended church assiduously, knows the hymns, prayers and benedictions used by the Catholic priests. In effect a pseudo-priest, the *pè-savann* is taken seriously by the faithful who need his services.

At the moment of the mystical marriage, he is introduced into the *oufò*, next to the *oungan,* to sing and bless the alliance of the *lwa* with his or her husband or wife. Witnesses come forward to place their signatures at the bottom of a marriage certificate that gives the names of the spouses (the follower and the *lwa*).

A special room in the *oufò* is reserved for the consecration of the marriage. During the dances and offerings, the *lwa* who has entered into marriage shows agreement by means of a crisis of possession that takes the human spouse. The *lwa* might also appear in the head of a participant in the ceremony or an initiate. The new spouse must devote a specific day of the week to his or her *lwa,* and on that day must abstain from sexual activity.

A colourful rug, ribbons of many colours hung from the ceiling, flowers on the altar and paintings on the walls – including that of the Virgin with halo, corresponding to the *lwa* Ezili – decorate the room reserved for the *lwa* by his or her spouse. The *lwa* often declare their desire for marriage through dreams, and sometimes through illness. In her painting *A Husband for Ezili* (below), Celestin Faustin shows the Virgin, satisfied with offerings of her favourite foods, disposed to receive her spouse, who wears a red shirt and opens his arms to her, as well as the many others who await her favours.

Subjected to persecution at the hands of both Church and state from the slave era, then to the repudiation of the majority of Haiti's intellectuals throughout the 19th century and until 1930, voodoo has displayed an astonishing capacity for survival. Far from aiding its cause, the political exploitation of the Duvalier regime tainted voodoo with evils formerly attributed to masters, slave dealers and colonials.

CHAPTER 7

AN ASTONISHING SURVIVAL

Seen in children wearing masks of devils or bulls during carnival, or a young woman emerging from a luck bath with the rooster she has sacrificed to Ogou – the imaginative power of voodoo is one of the most intrinsic cultural resources of the Haitian people.

At the edges of concealment

While not equally distributed throughout the land, the practice of voodoo remains deep-rooted in Haiti, especially in the Artibonite region in the middle of the country, where the largest temples have stood since the beginning of the 19th century, following on the heels of the proclamation of independence. The figure on how many people regularly practise voodoo continues to be elusive, as almost all call themselves Catholics. It is even said that the voodoo follower must be a Catholic, which recalls the history of voodoo's creation.

The penal code, which went into effect in 1835 under the presidency of Jean-Pierre Boyer, called for imprisonment of six months to two years for voodoo followers caught in the performance of 'superstitious' acts; these provisions remained in effect, virtually unchanged, until 1986. At regular intervals during this long period, government circulars encouraged the military leaders to lend a hand in the Church's fight against the voodoo societies.

Such a perpetual cloud of persecution pushed the voodoo faithful to create protective coverings. The priests got into the habit of allying themselves with the local leaders – the heads of the rural municipalities, who combined administrative, judicial and military powers. The same priests often belonged to secret societies or were known for their abilities in sorcery – two strong weapons against those who would attack their temples.

The political rehabilitation of voodoo by the dictator Duvalier

To ensure the long duration of his regime, President François Duvalier passed himself off as a zealous defender of the African element of Haitian culture. A former country doctor and ethnologist, in the 1940s he had published a series of articles in

François Duvalier (below, with his wife, in 1957) plunged his country into a thirty-year dictator-ship.

which he upheld the need to rehabilitate voodoo politically as the soul of the nation and the 'black' race, to which every 'authentic' Haitian leader should adhere as the source of his power.

From 1957 to 1971, 'Papa Doc' Duvalier succeeded in bringing into the service of his dictatorship many networks of *oungan,* whom he used as informers or agents of the secret military police known as the Tontons-macoutes. At the same time, he involved the government in the practice of voodoo, underwriting the ceremonies in order to gain the goodwill of the *lwa* and arouse the enthusiasm of the followers. With this backing, Papa Doc had the means to challenge the traditional powers of the Catholic Church, which he saw as the ally of the middle class and the 'mulatto' elite. On the other hand, the poorer classes experienced the Duvalier period as characterized by a power rooted in magic and sorcery – that is, in the negative aspects of voodoo.

The explosion of 'déchoukaj'

The day the regime fell, on 7 February 1986, a furious mob took the first steps towards the systematic destruction of all Duvalier's symbols.

With the Tontons-macoutes, a secret police modelled on the Nazis, Duvalier created a reign of terror, striking at anyone suspected of opposing his dictatorship. Above, Fritzner Lamour represented a Tonton-macoute with the head of a cock (the emblem of voodoo) on the body of a guinea fowl (an animal associated with the Maroons), referring to Duvalier's attempt to turn the forces of voodoo to his benefit. Above left, a parade of the flags begins a voodoo ceremony: the worshippers proceed with measured steps, closely following the customary protocol, under the protective shelter of the banners decorated with the colours of the *lwa*.

Servants of the *lwa* follow the custom of taking luck baths in an *oufò* or in the home, as well as in springs and rivers where *lwa* live. To prepare a luck bath at home requires various leaves, plants and herbs associated with the *lwa*, and thus having curative powers. To these might be added orgeat, perfume or jasmine flowers. The priest rubs this concoction on the individual while appealing to the *lwa* for protection. Strengthened by the spiritual qualities of the leaves and the good scent of the perfume that pleases the *lwa*, the individual can face his or her enemies with confidence. It is possible, however, for a worshipper to take more protection than is needed. Having too much 'luck' turns a person into a sorcerer (or a werewolf). Taking a luck bath is similar to buying spiritual powers which can turn on the purchaser with such force that they get out of control. The mud baths at Bassin-Saint-Jacques in the Plaine-du-Nord (left) are a destination of pilgrimages, as are Saut-d'Eau (opposite), with its immense waterfall lined with giant trees in which *lwa* live, and Villebonheur, favoured sites for the luck baths.

In Creole, this activity was labelled *déchoukaj,* which means uprooting.

Dozens of Tontons-macoutes were lynched or burned alive in the streets, among them many *oungan* accused of practising sorcery on behalf of the dictatorship. During the first three months following the departure of Jean-Claude 'Baby Doc' Duvalier, numerous Protestant ministers intensified their antivoodoo preaching by denouncing the *oungan* as responsible for the 'evil' that had spread throughout the country. They set off a new wave of looting against the *oufò.* The mob had been

The Duvaliers assumed power for life with the help of the Tontons-macoutes. Starting in 1985, the popular operation called *déchoukaj* undertook to remove all vestiges of the dictatorship. Macoutes and *oungan* were often lumped together. Thus one reads on the wall of a house in Port-au-Prince (above) 'an'n déchoké gangan' (destroy the *oungan*).

At Cap Haitien, the Tontons-macoutes fled under the protection of the army, while young people avid for vengeance and justice emptied their houses and burned all the contents (below, detail of a painting by Jean-Baptiste Jean showing *déchoukaj* in the city).

encouraged to confuse *oungan,* sorcerers and Tontons-macoutes.

With a view to the reestablishment of democracy, the new constitution, ratified on 29 March 1987, had to remove the traditional punishment for voodoo. In May of 1986 a two-day conference that brought together artists, intellectuals and educators around a group of priests, for the first time made a public statement against all persecution of voodoo practices. However, a division emerged among the temples as priests and initiates, no longer obliged to practise in secret, now had to choose whether to join in the struggle for democracy.

The moral campaign of the religious sects

The Protestant ministers – Baptists, Evangelists, Pentecostalists, Jehovah's Witnesses and Seventh-Day

Adventists – who preached against voodoo, calling it devil worship, all came from the United States. After making inroads on the poorest of the urban population, they began fanning out into the country-side. The Protestants do not take part in the spectacle

of burning the sacred objects of voodoo; instead, they bring forward voodoo followers who repent in public and confess to having made a covenant with the devil.

By passing off all the *lwa* as evil or satanic forces, the message of the Protestant sects revives the fantasy of sorcery. Even the conversions smack of ambiguity. For example, the new Protestant finds that the Bible is supposed to respond to his or her requests, even though not long before the same requests had been made of the *lwa*. At the same time, the system of voodoo beliefs continues to have an effect, as sickness, accidents and economic setbacks are invariably interpreted as punishments of the *lwa*. It is clear that the success of the Protestant sects points to a crisis.

S pearheading the struggle against the Tontons-macoutes, Jean-Bertrand Aristide came to be regarded as a prophet and champion of the poor people – small farmers, peddlers, and the unemployed of shantytowns – traditionally marginalized by the government. His election to the presidency in 1990 marked a break with a social system still based on old privileges, barely changed from the days of slavery. Above, a mural painting presents Aristide next to Toussaint-Louverture. Between them poses a young girl wearing the red kerchief of voodoo worshippers.

Voodoo in the light of day?

In a parallel to the demands for democracy voiced in 1791, the Reverend Jean-Bertrand Aristide came to power in 1990, having received sixty-seven per cent of the vote in the first free elections in the history of the country. To achieve these results, he rallied Catholics, Protestants and voodoo followers to his cause. The open coexistence of all three religions appeared on the horizon, even if the official statement of purpose worked against it; the Catholic hierarchy and the Protestant sects still viewed voodoo as a mass of superstitions that, sooner or later, had to be eradicated.

Likewise, the silence in education on the place of voodoo in Haiti's daily life reinforces not only the prejudices and stereotypes going back centuries but also the general illusions sustained about voodoo. It is almost as if the entire society suffers a kind of cultural schizophrenia. Thus, for example, on a political level, the *lwa* can bring people to power, and they are equally responsible for the unseating of a head of state. Even if they are marginalized, the priests can find comfort in the rumours

Under Aristide's presidency the ceremony of Bois-Caïman was commemorated for the first time in two hundred years, on 22 August 1991. However, protests by Protestant sects were arranged to coincide with this celebration, fomented by those who saw voodoo as the source of all the country's problems. At the same time, fear of democracy overwhelmed the traditional sources of power (the Church and army), resulting in a coup d'état on 29 September 1991 and Aristide's exile. After three years of military rule, he was reinstated as the legitimate president of Haiti on 15 October 1994.

of their abilities to manipulate the *lwa* in favour of certain political leaders.

There are further pressing questions to consider. Does religious freedom allow the inheritors of the voodoo cultural tradition to criticize as well as to celebrate the voodoo imaginary world? Does not voodoo have a tendency to draw its worshippers towards the past, placing them under the authority of tradition (symbolized by the dead, the ancestors, the *lwa*) rather than more flexible rules, subject to modern rational thinking? Voodoo's capacity for combining different beliefs does indeed indicate its openness to other systems.

A piece of worldwide cultural patrimony

In Benin, voodoo recently proved it is capable of filling the role of a positive

cultural and religious cement: the first world festival of the voodoo arts was held in Ouidah, in Benin, on 7–17 February 1993. Nearly one hundred societies from all over Africa, Cuba, Haiti, Trinidad and Brazil took part. For two weeks, parades of masqueraders, visits to ancient temples, spectacles and artistic demonstrations summed up the different expressions of voodoo under the African sun where it first saw light of day.

A whole assortment of prejudices held against voodoo has seemed to gradually disappear. Voodoo is, at one and the same time, the memory of a past in which God, humans and nature spoke the same language; the force of resistance against slavery in Haiti and throughout the New World, where the slave trade poured out its human cargo; and the ability to adapt to a great variety of situations.

It offers itself as the matrix of a civilization that, stretching from Africa to the Americas, participates in the heritage of universal culture. As in Ouidah, it has never disappeared in New York, Miami, the French West Indies, Guyana and even Paris – all the centres of the Haitian diaspora – where voodoo temples have been planted anew, and where the worship of the *lwa* does not place any obstacles to the adoption of new norms and practices.

In Ouidah, Benin, in 1993, members of voodoo societies and artists from all over the world gathered to remember the slave trade and slavery. The Africans (left and opposite, priests and dignitaries holding the decorated baton, symbol of sacred power), hosts of the great festival that witnessed all types of processions, felt themselves appointed the guardians of voodoo's place of origin. Tens of thousands of Haitians who emigrated from their native land, notably to the United States (above, a *manbo* officiating in her Brooklyn *oufò*), have continued to honour the *lwa*, recognizing in them powers that can help them as they endure the trials of a new life, far from their loved ones and their country.

DOCUMENTS

1988

The spelling used in this book, voodoo, reflects the common English-language usage. However, numerous contemporary authors have chosen the spelling *vodou*, to emphasize the African origins of the religion, or the better-known transcription *vaudou*, used since the 18th century in narratives and historical and anthropological works. In the main text of the book, words from the Creole language have been rendered in the phonetic spellings officially adopted in Haiti several years ago. In the following extracts, there are variations in spelling which have been retained as in the original.

The devil, voodoo and the missionaries

'Residents who buy newly arrived slaves must inform the governors and intendants of the said islands within a week at latest under penalty of immediate fine. The governors will give the necessary orders for the baptism and instruction of the slaves within a suitable period.' In 1685, the Black Code thus instituted the necessary purification by baptism. Missionaries and travellers affirmed that not only was the measure inadequate, it also fed into the practice of African superstitions.

Previous pages: *Loa* (p. 128), a painting by Denis Smith. Prospère Pierre Louis, drawing of the *lwa* (p. 129), 1988.

No baptism for sorcerers

Father Jean-Baptiste Labat, a Dominican missionary of the end of the 17th century, told how slaves combined Catholic observance with their African beliefs, which he considered pure sorcery and devil worship.

It was about that time that a Negro slave belonging to one of my parishioners, Monsieur Philippes Mignac, came to me asking me to return a certain small sack that I had taken from him before I baptized him. I had been warned by his master that he had a hand in sorcery; he located lost objects; he foretold the future; he predicted the arrival of ships, and other things to come, by the same means as the devil, and revealed to him by the latter. As I have never placed much credence in such things, I thought of the Negro as a charlatan who imposed on simple folk to relieve them of their money. However, having questioned him carefully, I realized there was some truth to what I had been told....
I baptized him after making him renounce all the pacts, implicit or explicit, he might have made with the devil. I directed his master, who was also his godfather, to watch his conduct carefully. For three months I was extremely pleased with him; no one was more punctual than he when it came to the Mass and the Catechism: he urged me to permit him to receive Communion, and I began to think about it, convincing myself that the Baptism had lifted entirely from his mind all notions of his former calling: Then one Sunday morning I found him at my door holding a chicken in each hand. I thought he wanted to sell them, and asked him the price; he answered

that he wanted to give them to me as a present; I thanked him and refused to take them without paying something. After some formalities, he told me he did not want money at all; but if I would like to return his small sack I would do him a great kindness.

That request pained me greatly; I knew he wanted to go back to his former activities. Meanwhile, in order to delve more closely into his heart, I pretended to have no problem granting his request. I questioned him on the use he made of the different objects in the sack: he told me all I wished to know, and then confessed that since it had been taken from him he had become destitute and miserable, whereas before he had been very well off, because those who came to consult him paid him handsomely. He told me more than I needed to discover that his heart was perverted. Therefore I changed my tone of voice and, after giving him a fierce scolding, I threatened to place him in the hands of the law, which would not fail to have him burned alive: and to make him realize he would never have his sack, I told my Negro to go find it and burn it on the spot. It was brought to me: but since my little Negro had been taken with the gewgaws, he had abstracted some of them, including a grotesque figure in terra cotta, which was the idol that the Negro consulted, and which he assured me answered all the questions he put to him.

Jean-Baptiste Labat
Nouveaux Voyages aux Isles Françaises
d'Amérique, 1722

The 'frenetic ceremonies of these convulsive types'

Michel-Etienne Descourtilz, who visited Saint-Domingue after the slave rebellion

of 1791, considered voodoo an idolatrous sect that carried out vengeful practices by means of magic.

Having heard a great deal about an idolatrous sect called *vaudoux* [*sic*] at Saint-Domingue, and whose gatherings were taking place at our habitation, I had brought to me a trusted Negress who, after regaling me with supernatural happenings, gave me an eyewitness account of the frenetic ceremonies of these convulsive types. 'The *vaudoux*', said the truthful Finette, 'are of different nations…. Reunited on the ground that must be the theatre of their convulsive grimaces, they smile as they meet, jostle rudely, and there you have two in crisis, feet in the air, howling like the wild beasts, and foaming like them.

'One day', she continued, 'I passed two of these convulsive types, and either because their proselytes wanted to give standing to their system, or because with these unimpeachable proofs they wanted to take advantage of my young age by initiating me into their mysteries, they introduced me into the circle, and one of them was ordered, by the leader of the band, to take a lit coal that was given to him, and it seemed not to burn him in the least; another to have strips of flesh removed with iron nails, which was carried out, without my noticing the least sign of awareness.

'Dompète (that's the name of the all-powerful leader of the fanatic band), they told me, had the power to see with his own eyes, whatever the material obstacle, no matter the distance; a fictitious ability, made up to get the better of the credible and lord it over the doubtful, whose lack of confidence is punished by a poison familiar to them and, in the hands of Dompète, used daily and with impunity.

'The acolytes of that sect also possess the magical means to exact vengeance. Has a man suffered harshly at the hands of his lover, or the unfaithfulness of his mistress? A ray's stinger thrown into the guilty party's urine will avenge his anger, by striking the faithless one with a languishing illness, which the *vaudoux* can end at will with a different preparation.'

Michel-Etienne Descourtilz
Voyages d'un Naturaliste
1809

The worship of the sacred snake

Veiled behind the accounts of sorcery in the writings of the first missionaries and administrators, voodoo was given its first visual description in a work by Moreau de Saint-Méry, written in 1797.

According to the Arada Negroes, who are the true followers of Voodoo in the Colony, and who maintain its principles and laws, Voodoo means an all-powerful and supernatural being, who is the source of all the events that take place on the earth.
This being is a nonvenomous snake, or a species of serpent, under whose auspices gather all who share the faith. Knowledge of the past, the science of the present, foreknowledge of the future, all of this the snake possesses, and it consents to communicate its power solely through the medium of a high priest whom the adherents choose, or of a Negress, which the latter through his love has elevated to the rank of high priestess....

Gatherings of the true Voodoo, that which has retained the greatest degree of its primitive purity, take place only in secret, once the night's shadow has fallen, and in a cloistered place safe from the eyes of the profane. There, each initiate puts on a pair of sandals, and places around his body a more or less considerable number of kerchiefs of the colour red or predominantly of that tone. The King of Voodoo has the most beautiful and greatest number of kerchiefs, and those completely red and that circle his forehead are his diadem. A cord, usually blue, marks him out in striking dignity.

Once it has been verified that no curious onlooker has managed to penetrate the enclosure, the ceremony is begun with the worship of the snake, with avowals to remain faithful to its cult and to submit to all of its orders. The oath of secrecy, the very basis of the society, is reaffirmed, between the hands of the King and Queen, and it is accompanied by the most horrible things that delirium is capable of imagining, to make it more imposing....

It is natural to believe that Voodoo owes its origins to the worship of the snake, to which the inhabitants of Ouidah are particularly given, and who say it comes from the kingdom of Ardra, from the same Slave Coast....

L.-E. Moreau de Saint-Méry
Description topographique, physique, civile, politique et historique de la partie française de l'île de Saint-Dominique
1797

'How the Carib Priests Worked Up Courage', in B. Picard, *L'Histoire générale des cérémonies*, 1673.

The antisuperstitious campaigns

In 1860 the Church signed a concordat with the Haitian government recognizing Catholicism as the official state religion. Soon it started to persecute voodoo.

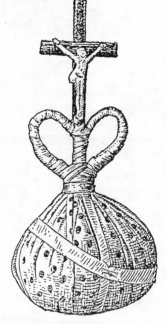

T he sacred objects of voodoo bring together pagan and Christian symbols, God and Satan, as complementary forces.

'A small Guinea transplanted in America': a disgrace

Magic, sorcery and superstitions were vigorously denounced during a conference held by the bishop of Cap Haitien in August 1896. It was felt that voodoo had made a mockery of civilized people and only a holy war could succeed against it.

It is certain that we cannot heap enough dishonour on these presumptuous and shameful observances, unworthy of civilized people, sinful to Christians. This insane confidence in practices and objects devoid of any virtue in themselves, much less any conferred by God or his Church; this overblown or ridiculous power attributed to saints, to images, to relics, and invoked, often enough, to achieve criminal ends; these claims to create supernatural effects by methods condemned by religion and common sense, these are so many violations against the purity of the faith, so many offences to the saints, so many outrages against God himself.

Meanwhile, would to God that we do not find ourselves more serious subjects to lament! But we are in a struggle with idolatry. Numerous Haitians offer to their imaginary gods the sovereign worship owed to the sole Creator, and you know, my brothers, how this plague has spread these last years!…

How can I describe the injury done to our national honour by our attachments to old African observances? I need courage to answer that question; take courage, then, to listen to me. A Dominican newspaper stated in 1892 that Haiti was the only American power that still had African magicians and dances, and concluded that Haiti is a small Guinea transplanted in America, and the disgrace of the American countries. This is what others have the right to say about us; and you know that it is not the worst that is said....

A few words to recap, and then I am done. The Haitian nation is sick, profoundly sick; it is suffering from paganism; the illness, it is true, does not have strong roots in the soul of the people; nonetheless, it tires it out, it disturbs it, it saps its strength, like those slow fevers that seem harmless at first but exhaust the sick person and end by leading him to the tomb. Also, our sickness is a shameful sickness, it dishonours us even more than it ravages us. As long as voodoo exists among us, we cannot pretend to pass for a truly civilized nation. Therefore, whatever the cost, we must get rid of this tumour, we must wage pitiless war against this army of brigands, called *bocors,* whose existence alone brings us disgrace. I do not want to leave these premises without enlisting all of you in the combat against these public enemies.

Bishop of Cap Haitien,
August 1896

Refuse this ignoble 'mixture'

For Monsignor Robert, Bishop of Gonaïves, the great 'antisuperstitious campaign' of 1941 delivered the Haitian people from Satan's tyranny.

The results obtained revealed the depth of the disease, the breadth of the deviation and the amplitude of the encroachment, which we could only suspect. Compelled to renounce completely their superstition in order to take part in the Sacraments, eighty per cent of those who communicated preferred to give up Communion instead. All of these can thus be numbered among those who practise that abomination designated in Creole by a word that transmits total horror: 'the mixture'. They think they can set together truth and lies, ignoring Saint Paul's command: 'Do not mix God and Belial' ['And what concord hath Christ with Belial?' 2 Corinthians, 6:15]; they think they can serve God and Satan at the same time, even giving the better part of their devotion to the demon, since in making a choice, they chose the latter.

In responding to our call, you have made an enormous contribution to the establishment of the rule of God here. It is your breaking ties with ignoble superstition and that horrible 'mixture' that made it possible for us to see where we stood at this point. It is in agreeing to take this oath that you have allowed us to disperse the sacrileges committed by thousands of false Catholics who dare communicate all the while continuing to 'serve the *lwa*'. Finally, it is thanks to you that we will be able to carry out our effort to reestablish the truth and thus open the road to salvation to so many souls that groan under the tyranny of Satan and know not how they can find the way to free themselves.

Msgr Robert, Bishop of Gonaïves,
pastoral letter, 2 February 1941

'One does not cook cucumber with aubergine': a catechism from the same campaign

The job of eradicating voodoo, which the religious authorities had undertaken, was waged with a catechism in the form of a pamphlet that provided simple questions and answers, perhaps read aloud in

unison by the new penitents, and enumerated all the details of voodoo worship in order to condemn them clearly.

You come to catechism to rid yourself of all the old beliefs from Africa, then to learn how the true religion of the Good Lord works.

Q: The Africa that you found at your birth, does it work with the religion of the Good Lord?

A: No. Africa does not work with religion.

Q: Why does Africa not work with the religion of the Good Lord?

A: Africa cannot work with the religion of the Good Lord because Africa is the *lwa,* and the religion of the Good Lord is the Good Lord. One does not cook cucumber with aubergine.

Q: Who is Jesus Christ?

A: Jesus Christ is God. Thus, he is the Saviour. It is he who has suffered, who died so we could leave Africa.

Q: How do you recognize the rebellious angels?

A: The rebellious angels appear in strength during our sleep to seduce our good angel. They come to sing, they come to dance in our head. They say they are our masters. They say that they are the papas, that it has fallen to them to cure us. They promise many riches. They ask for food and dancing. They ask for 'food for the dead', candles, images, crucifixes, rosaries, rogations, armchairs, dishes, clothing, kerchiefs. They say we must do penance, offer up prayers, make pilgrimages.

Q: Why can't the children of African Guinea be stronger than the children of the Good Lord?

A: The children of African Guinea cannot be stronger than the children of the Good Lord because they are slaves of the *lwa;* even worse, they commit many sins and will go to hell.

'Yes, with all my strength, I renounce': the oath of the 'rejectors'

In the churches, at the conclusion of a long dialogue with the priest, each worshipper was called on to affirm, with an oath of 'rejection', that he or she was giving up voodoo practices forever.
The end of the questioning preceding the official renunciation follows:

31. Who is the principal slave of Satan?

A: The principal slave of Satan is the *oungan.*

32. What is the name that the *oungan* give to Satan?

A: The names that the *oungan* give to Satan are *lwa,* angels, saints, the dead, *marassa.*

33. Why do the *oungan* take the names of angels, saints and the dead and give them to Satan?

A: The *oungan* take the names of angels,

saints, and the dead and give them to Satan in order to deceive us more easily.
34. How do people serve Satan?
A: In sinning, in casting spells, practising magic, *manjé-lwa, manjé-le-zanj, manjé-marassa.*
37. Do we have the right to mix with the slaves of Satan?
A: No, because they are evildoers, they are liars like Satan.

THE PRIEST: 'Do you today and forever renounce superstitious practices?'
THE REJECTOR: 'Yes, with all my strength, I renounce.'
THE PRIEST: 'Do you renounce the religion of Africa?'
THE REJECTOR: 'Yes, with all my strength, I renounce.'

Text of the oath of the 'rejector':

I before God stand in the Tabernacle, before the priest who represents Him and renew the promises of my baptism. With hand on the Gospels I swear never to give a food-offering [*mangerloa*] of whatever kind – never to attend a Voodoo ceremony of whatever kind, never to take part in a service to *loa* in any way whatsoever.

I promise to destroy or have destroyed as soon as possible all fetishes and objects of superstition, if any – on me, in my house, and in my compound.

Partial view of the crowd assembled at Saint-Michel de l'Attalaye on 8 February 1942 for a great celebration during the antisuperstitious campaign. 'Thousands of people came to find …a freedom and a peace they cannot get from voodoo.'

M.M., priest of Saint-Jacques

In short I swear never to sink to any superstitious practice whatever.
[For married persons] I promise moreover to bring up my children without exception in the Catholic and Roman religion, outside all superstition, submitting myself fully to the teaching of this Holy Church.
And I promise that with God's help I shall abide by my oath until death.

Alfred Métraux
Voodoo in Haiti, 1972

'The Cross versus the rattle'

In 1960, in a book entitled La Croix contre l'asson, *Father Carl Edward Peters assessed the antisuperstitious campaign, in which, in his role as missionary, he had taken an active part. He points out how the campaign saved the country from Satan, honoured in the voodoo religion, as well as how it represented for the Church a process of cleansing and purifying the Catholic religion.*

We must truly destroy everything: break the bottles and jugs, rip up the images, pull out and burn the post and the cross, carry away the stones, take away the necklaces, crush the *caye-loas,* cut the worshipped wood, desecrate all that reeks of the superstitious 'service'. At first, it will seem painful, but it is the people who will remain. And they will not take us seriously if we are not strict.

At the beginning, it must be the Father himself who will accomplish this job. The people will not do it because of their fear.... And one hears the following kinds of remarks: 'I won't go and get the priest, but I'll be happy if he comes.'...

Once the movement is under way, it is absolutely impossible for the Father to go everywhere and destroy superstitious objects, to 'clean' the country and its habitations. But it has always been possible to find, according to one's needs, the necessary recruits, starting with the sacristans....

At the end of December 1945, Father Rémy Augustin, writing on the subject of this cleanup, explained it thus: 'There was a kind of delirium to it, the joy of deliverance was so contagious.' In this delirium there were a few unfortunate episodes, some overzealous tactics for which the clergy was held responsible. Personally, I witnessed no such instances, but I know that here and there the 'rejectors' forced the 'nonrejectors' to give up their fetishes.... Let us then check a delirious mob. Let us then preach calm to these people who believe themselves to be freed from a true slavery and desire to fix firmly the acquired gains or to secure the same joy for their brothers. Some abuses are inevitable, but there is nothing in the regulations

of the campaign to prove that the bishops encouraged these abuses.

Carl Edward Peters
La Croix contre l'asson, 1960

CARL EDWARD PETERS
MONTFORTAIN

La Croix
CONTRE
l'Asson

Imprimerie LA PHALANGE
Port-au-Prince, Haiti.
1960

'Catholicism too is integral to Vodouisants' lives'

If Catholicism is identified with heaven, Vodou is associated with the earth. And if Haitian writers say that the lwas 'have to do with the earth', and hence cannot be uprooted from Haitian life, it is because Vodou fulfills important functions in Haitian society that are distinct from those of Catholicism. Aside from its healing power through magic, it maintains the vision and the hope of the lwas' assistance in enabling its devotees to cope with the poverty and famine caused by the incessant erosion of arable soil by the torrential rainfall of the tropics. Moreover, the oungans and mambos are powerful individuals in Haitian society, for they do not merely officiate at Vodou ceremonies, but fulfill important civic as well as political functions which the Catholic priests cannot perform. Often, local authorities will call upon Vodou priests to furnish character references on behalf of members of the community.

But Catholicism too is integral to Vodouisants' lives. Apart from the social services provided by its schools and hospitals, its rituals offer a means through which its communicants can participate in Haiti's official culture. Their children's baptisms, confirmation, and first communions, their marriages and funeral masses, provide occasions for social intercourse. And it serves, as it did in the formative years of the republic, as a means by which Haiti maintains contact with the outside, providing opportunities to participate with other nations in common international ventures.

Because of the importance of both Vodou and Catholicism to Haitians, it is doubtful that either of them will ever disappear from the country – but the continued contact between them may produce changes in both…if Haitian society remains stable, and if the country's political life is free of revolutions, it is possible that syncretism may develop between the two religions in the future. This possibility is strengthened by the ecumenical spirit of Vatican II, and by the overwhelming support given to the Salesian Father Jean-Bertrand Aristide ('Titid') by voters during the December 1990 presidential election. Aristide's government lasted merely nine months; it was toppled on 30 September 1991, by a military coup. But the complex issues that initiated the coup did not change the fact that, since 1986, the Haitian clergy has had to acknowledge Vodou as a vital force in Haitian political and social life, and its oungans and mambos as powerful and influential figures in Haitian religious life. Haiti's March 1987 Constitution guarantees religious freedom to all its citizens, and hence legally grants to Vodou a status equal to that of the church.

The provisions of the new constitution have helped to foster an atmosphere of religious openness throughout the country in recent years – an openness in which Vodouisants have enjoyed a religious freedom reminiscent of the days of Faustin Soulouque. On a recent trip to Haiti, I heard what was perhaps one of the rare moments in Haitian history: the radio and television programs broadcasting general news about religion included events, not only in the life of the church (both Catholic and Protestant), but those of Vodou as well. Moreover, a significant change in the church has recognized the talents of Haitian artists, even though many of them are Vodouisants. Many parishes have allowed local artists to paint biblical scenes on the walls of church sanctuaries. These murals are colorful representations of Haitian life. Christ, the saints, and the apostles are black; they are depicted amidst the towns and cities of the country, even near what appear to be ounfos.

Leslie G. Desmangles
The Faces of the Gods: Vodou and Roman Catholicism in Haiti
1992

How the *lwa* show themselves to humans

Each lwa *is tied to a specific realm of nature (air, earth, water or fire), tree or plant, human behaviour, colour and ritual. Voodoo followers identify them by means of these specific signs.*

P rospère Pierre Louis, drawing of the *lwa*, 1987.

NAMES	LEGBA
RITES	Rada
COLOURS	Red
PREFERRED TREES	Calabash, *Cirouellier, Médicinier (Tatropha cureas)*
TYPES OF POSSESSION	Brutality, force, violence
OFFERINGS	Cassava, rice, green banana, smoked foods, mottled cock
ATTRIBUTIONS	Protector of the home
CHARACTERISTICS	Interpreter of the *lwa*; keeper of the gates, crossroads, and paths; rival of Dambala
HABITATION	Gates and crossroads; *médicinier*
CATHOLIC COUNTERPARTS	Saint Peter (keys) or Saint Anthony (lost objects)
REALMS	Earth
SYMBOLS	Feeble old man in rags
SPECIAL DAYS	Friday, Saturday

AZAKA	GÉDÉ	BARON SAMDI	DAMBALA
Rada	Rada and Petro	Rada and Petro	Rada
Blue, red, green	Black, purple, white	Black, purple	White
Cherry *(Malphigia ureus)* Banana	*Médicinier* Calabash	*Médicinier* Citron	All trees, especially the cotton tree and the silk tree; also the calabash, palmetto, tamarind
Peasant dress; the possessed wears a straw hat, blue shirt and trousers and red neckerchief, carries a straw satchel	Obscene words and gestures; cadaverous appearance	Macabre and obscene	Imitation of a snake's movements
Corn, bread, unrefined sugar, brandy	Black goat, black cock	Salted herring, black goat, black hens	Everything white: hens, rice, milk, eggs
Harvest	Making or repelling spells	?	Wealth, luck, happiness
Peasant *lwa,* cultivator of fields and agriculture; distrustful, sly, greedy; they hate townspeople	*Lwa* of the dead	Head of the Gédé (*lwa* of the dead)	Principle of goodness
Fields	Cemeteries and subterranean places	Cross at the entrance to cemeteries	Springs and rivers
Saint Isidore	Saint Expedit	?	Saint Patrick represented chasing the snakes from Ireland
Earth	Earth	Earth	Water
Mabouya (small reptile)	Cadaver, black cross; farm implements	Tall, black clothes	Snake-rainbow
Friday, Saturday	Monday, Friday	Saturday	Thursday

NAMES	AYIDA WEDO	EZILI	OGOU FERAY
RITES	Rada	Rada	Rada
COLOURS	Blue, white	Blue, pink	Red
PREFERRED TREES	All trees, especially the cotton tree and the silk tree; also the calabash, palmetto, tamarind	*Cirouellier* Laurel	Calabash Pine
TYPES OF POSSESSION	Imitation of a snake's movements	Seductive air and provocative behaviour; seeks perfumes	Brusque, coarse and authoritative language
OFFERINGS	Everything white: hens, rice, milk, eggs	Toiletries; rare and refined dishes, rice, chicken	Red cock, bull
ATTRIBUTIONS	Wealth, luck, happiness	Love	Fighting against miserable conditions
CHARACTERISTICS	Wife of Dambala	Mulatto, coquette, sensual; beauty and grace, luxury and pleasure; promiscuous	Warrior and soldier
HABITATION	Springs and rivers	River banks	Calabash tree, bamboo
CATHOLIC COUNTERPARTS	Our Lady of the Immaculate Conception	The Virgin Mary	Saint James the Greater
REALMS	Water	Water	Fire
SYMBOLS	Snake-rainbow	Heart, mirror	A sabre driven into the earth
SPECIAL DAYS	Monday, Tuesday	Tuesday, Thursday	Friday, Saturday, Monday

AGWE	SIMBI
Rada	Petro
White, green, pink	Black, grey
Raisinier (cocolota uvifera)	Mango, calabash, elm
Seeking water for diving and swimming	The possessed throws him- or herself into a pond or a river
White sheep, hens; fine drink: champagne	Black or grey animals: pig, goat, guinea fowl, turkey, hen
Protection of navigation and shipping; fishing	Gift of clairvoyance
Mulatto, fair skin, sea-green eyes; naval officer	Guardian of springs and ponds
Sea	Springs, caves, mountains
Saint Ulrich	The Magi
Water	Water
Boat, oars	Pond
Thursday	Tuesday, Thursday, Friday

This chart of classifications and correspondences contains only some of the major lwa *of the Rada and Petro rites. The* lwa *of the Kongo rites are celebrated collectively, at the* lakou *Nan Soukri, near the town of Gonaïves. They alone represent what is called an 'escort', led by the* lwa *Man Inan, wife of Bazou Mennen, by whom she had 101 children. Considered something like a queen mother, Man Inan is associated with Our Lady of the Assumption, her Catholic counterpart. She is celebrated, with her entire escort, or retinue, every year on 15 August. The Kongo* lwa *are considered the* lwa-gad *(guards), and they guarantee protection to their servants in the difficult moments of their lives.*

Prospère Pierre Louis, drawing of the *lwa*, 1986.

For the rehabilitation of voodoo

A remnant of colonialism, the label of 'superstition' clings to voodoo even today. Ethnologists and sociologists from Haiti have proposed conferring a more dignified status: religion, culture and spiritual principle that, tying people to their origins, allows them to find a place in the world.

Gabriel Bien-Aimé, *Oungan*, 1985.

'Voodoo is a religion'

An early champion of the Négritude movement, Jean Price-Mars vigorously criticized the tendency then in vogue among Haitian intellectuals to adulate French culture and proposed the rehabilitation of voodoo as a religion, as an essential part of Haiti's national culture and as a religion worthy of study. Despite Duvalier's sinister use of the 'African aspect' later on, Price-Mars contributed to a new questioning of the Haitian identity.

Voodoo is a religion because all its adherents believe in the existence of spiritual beings who live anywhere in the universe in close intimacy with humans whose activity they dominate....

Voodoo is a religion because the cult appertaining to its gods requires a hierarchical priestly body, a society of the faithful, temples, altars, ceremonies, and finally a whole oral tradition which has certainly not come down to us unaltered, but thanks to which the essential elements of this worship have been transmitted.

Voodoo is a religion because, amid the confusion of legends and the corruption of fables we can discern a theology, a system of representation thanks to which our African ancestors have, primitively, accounted for natural phenomena and which lies dormantly at the base of the anarchical beliefs upon which the hybrid Catholicism of our popular masses rests.

We are aware that this statement will bring quick objection. You are, no doubt, wondering what is the moral value of such a religion and, as your religious education is dominated by the efficiency of the Christian moral philosophy, you use that as your standard of judgment.

In the light of such rules you can only dutifully condemn Voodoo as a religion, not only because you reproach it for being immoral but, more logically, because you frankly declare it amoral. And since it is not known how an amoral religion can exist, you cannot accept Voodoo as a religion. Ah! Such an attitude would be worse than an intellectual injustice, it would be a negation of intelligence. For, in the end, we are aware that every religion has its moral code and that it is most often closely related to the mental evolution of the group in which this religion has been born and has taken root.

Jean Price-Mars
So Spoke the Uncle, trans. M. W. Shannon, 1983

A manufactured rift

Jacques Roumain, Communist writer and author, was the founder of the Bureau of Ethnology of Port-au-Prince in 1934. He was one of the very few Haitian intellectuals who dared to denounce the antisuperstitious campaign of 1941.

From 1804 to the date of the Concordat [1860], in a country with a scattered rural population, lacking roads, schools, hospitals, it would have been astonishing if the coating of Catholicism were not very thin and always ready to peel off the older stock of African beliefs.

But how does it come about that from 1860 to today, during eighty-two years, with a certified clergy whose means are never lacking, a better system of communication, a much larger distribution of religious and lay instruction, churches in every town and suburb, rural chapels, [and] tighter administrative and cultural

Georges Liautaud, *Ogoun*, 1980.

connections, coherent and continuous between town and country – how does it come about that a resounding failure of Catholic evangelism is confessed, and that the fault is laid solely to the Haitian people, represented as a dark, primitive mass given over entirely to irreducible superstitions?

We have shown that the Haitian peasant is no more superstitious or backward than a Breton or Tyrolean peasant of the same economic circumstances....

The 'antisuperstitious' campaign gave rise to painful debates and revealed a rift in the unity of the Haitian people at a time that demands a serious and undivided mustering of our forces. I believe this discord to be artificial and manufactured. To what purpose? We shall find out.

It is the political significance of the last incidents, the problems they pose, the solutions they impose, that guide our conduct and our thinking. It costs us little to speak the truth. To the question that public opinion has expressed with amazement: what is the reason for the failure of Catholic evangelism in Haiti? there is an answer: this failure does not exist. The clergy in itself is not altogether guilty for the coagulation of voodoo. There are, undoubtedly, among the Catholic priests serious missionaries who are deeply affected by their great spiritual responsibility. I have known many worthy of admiration. And rascals, too.

At a time when national unity is essential in the fight against the Nazi menace, the Haitian people are divided into 'rejectors' and 'nonrejectors', into Protestant and Catholic.

While our national defence is a direct and vital function of good relations between the two Republics that share sovereignty over the Island, the Dominican people are being set against the Haitian people.

We believe that this so-called superstitious campaign has hidden motives, subtle and political, that do not appear on the surface. One cannot underestimate the fact that the French Catholic hierarchy is pro-Vichy, pro-collaborationist, anti-British, anti-Soviet, anti-Allies: in short, that it is part of the pro-Fascist machinery.

That is a brutal fact. In Haiti, it managed to escape the notice of many patriotic French priests of good faith – but it does not make it any the less undeniable.

Jacques Roumain
A propos de la campagne antisuperstitieuse,
Port-au-Prince, 1942

Emerging from chaos by means of the *lwa*: voodoo and therapy

In a work entitled Dieu dans le vaudou haïtien, *Laënnec Hurbon referred to the work of two psychiatrists of Port-au-Prince, Louis Mars and L. Bijou, who studied many cases of voodoo followers with schizophrenia.*

Persecution by the spirit poses a question to voodoo followers, and they are, as it were, linked together by this question. It concerns fate: the *lwa* is a foreign power, unknown and anonymous, that pounces on the individual, who can only regain his or her balance by renewing a dialogue with him. In calling the *lwa*, in giving him the kind of worship that pleases him, the voodoo follower gains his protection. She or he no longer lives in nonsense and confusion. She or he recognizes her/his proper place in the group, the place of others, and of all the things of the universe. The dialogue renewed with the *lwa* means sense restored. For the voodoo follower, it does not exist outside what is offered by custom or tradition. The *lwa* are…the foundations and the cohesion of the cultural social group. To be deprived of dialogue with them is to be deprived of dialogue with the community, it is to be consigned to individuality, to insecurity, to anonymity, to death.

However, in Haiti the conflicts of classes, languages, religions eat so deeply into the body of voodoo followers that obeying tradition is always more or less fettered. What happens when, following a conversion to Catholicism or Protestantism and the pressure of Western values, service to the *lwa* is neglected? We are witness to a reinforcement of persecutory interpretations by the *lwa*. Louis Mars, who works with the clinical problems of voodoo, has realized that a third of the mentally ill in a portion of the middle and lower classes – that is, in populations that have neither completely left the peasant class nor become well integrated into the urban world – suffered mostly from paranoid schizophrenia. At the same time, paranoid schizophrenia presented by Louis Mars. The first thing to strike him, he explains, is her indifference to everything around her. She knows full well she is in Port-Beudet, yet she does not trouble herself to know what the people around her are doing, does not demand to eat or to go out, does not know the name of the nurse who cares for her, nor of the doctor who submits her to repeated examinations, nor of

Luck bath at Bassin-Saint-Jacques.

according to L. Bijou, from April 1959 to June 1960, sixty per cent of the out-patients and sixty-eight per cent of the inpatients of the psychiatric centre were schizophrenics. From April 1960 to March 1961, sixty-nine per cent of the inpatients were diagnosed with schizophrenia. Without any doubt, schizophrenics constitute the lion's share of the clientele of *bocors* and herb doctors.

To give an example, here is the case of a young woman suffering from the employees of the asylum she meets in the ward, in the clinic, in the courtyard, she does not ask to see her parents and affects the greatest indifference towards her mother. To questions about her she answers, 'I don't know. She is not dead. She is there or she isn't there!' She claims that she is going to be poisoned, that a being inside her – the spirit of a saint – is persecuting her; and she uses expressions randomly in English, French and Creole.

It is not our intention to present here an examination of this clinical case. We

G abriel Bien-Aimé, *Grande Brigitte and Baron Samdi*, 1988.

wish only to show how the loss of the symbolic language of the spirits dooms the individual voodoo follower who has not been integrated into modern society, the impossibility of finding her way again, to place herself in the world and in a social group. In the example we cited, the young woman did not manage to recover the laws of time and space, she no longer knows where she is. She recognizes neither her father nor her mother. For her, language no longer means anything, except the pursuit of her own emptiness. Also, she is where she speaks her language. Properly speaking, speech in her is chained up, and ultimately encysted in her own body, like something that persecutes her. Some troubled voodoo followers have demons taking over their bodies, removing all its substance and reducing it to powerlessness.

How do such individuals recover their place in the world? It often happens that conversion to Protestantism or Catholicism, or simply access to the values of modern society, is never complete enough to give the former voodoo faithful a code that allows them to restructure their personality. 'In all cases', remarks Dr Louis Mars, 'the cultural material that clothes the delirium is broken into small fragments. Each piece nonetheless reflects a certain image, twisted and deforming of the culture, much as fragments of a mirror do not cease to project the light of the sun. Each cultural characteristic is separated from its context and used by the patient's subjectivity.'

Only the reintegration of custom can furnish the individual with the meanings necessary for his re-equilibration. Since the illness is a question posed by the *lwa,* the sick person must conform anew to the symbolism of the *lwa,* offering them sacrificial ceremonies to appease them. In effect, it is through this submission to the *lwa* that the individual can emerge from formlessness and confusion, learn again the place of things and beings in the universe. The *lwa* represent, we have seen, a mode of articulation of the real and the social, and of the self in the real and the social. The novice voodoo follower who is going to be possessed

G abriel Bien-Aimé, *Master of the Earth*, 1988.

by a *lwa* views the first jolts of the trance as a passing madness: the *lwa,* it is said, is not yet settled in the head. Under the direction of the *oungan,* a ceremony will be organized in honour of a *lwa* for his recognition, his appointment and submission to his orders. This is also one of the meanings of initiation: it readjusts perfectly the faithful to their *lwa,* like the horse to its rider. In this way, the voodoo follower recovers his or her identity. In Western society, however, the person would be sent to the asylum – as, indeed, happened in the first place with our young woman who found herself in a psychiatric centre, an institution of the Western type. Here in voodoo, thanks to common beliefs shared by a social group, the delirium of our 'sick' young woman could be expressed freely. For the voodoo follower, the universe of spirits becomes the means of expression of the drama of recognition. Presenting a sacrifice to the *lwa,* submitting to the interdictions of the *lwa,* this is to allow the presence of the other to penetrate desire, to cease to let oneself be carried away, seized by one's own transparent image, to have access to speech.

Laënnec Hurbon
Dieu dans le vaudou haïtien, 1987

Gabriel Bien-Aimé, *Ezili's Thoughts,* 1988.

A profound experience of the human condition and a desire to transcend it

The population of voodoo followers find themselves surrounded on every side, by the State, which actually uses voodoo to better consolidate its regime; by Catholicism, which holds its power over voodoo's head; by American Protestantism, which lays siege to the lower classes to better control them; and by the elite and the bourgeoisie, which are dominated by Western ideologies and which see in voodoo either a primitive situation…or a folk-lore that can be placed in a showcase and offered to slake the foreigners' thirst for exoticism. But, like a town under siege, voodoo struggles….

Does voodoo have a future? That is the same as asking if the Creole language has a future. In truth, the future of voodoo is the future of the exploited Haitian masses. Voodoo is not in itself a cause of underdevelopment. It is rather the expression of a distress whose solution lies elsewhere than in voodoo; elsewhere, meaning a level of political combat to which the exploited classes must find access. In the course of this political combat, new forms of expression of the masses will appear, new lines will be drawn up, a new culture will emerge, but always based on existing potentialities.

What remains clear is that voodoo cannot be reduced to a purely social and political alienation.

Laënnec Hurbon
Dieu dans le vaudou haïtien, 1987

Voodoo in art

Having created an invisible world and forged the identity of Haiti's black people, voodoo naturally found its way into the arts. Its power finds expression in literature and dance, and in the art that has led critics to say that Haiti's soil gave rise to a 'people of painters'.

W rought-iron cross figure used in the worship of voodoo.

Seducing the African muse

While voodoo was still being denounced everywhere, Antoine Innocent in 1906 used it in a positive context, in a novel entitled Mimola.

Frè Ti Dor had a singular physiognomy, bushy hair, eyes glowing like two embers, two small circles of gold in his ears, the way everyone was wearing them at the time; on his fingers, numerous rings set with stones of every shade. He seemed ill at ease in his clothes: a suit of coarse blue linen. He wore a hat made of thick wool with a band of floss silk, slippers made of goatskin, and socks with holes that allowed one to notice that the trousers were too short. His voice was sometimes refined, sometimes coarse: an oddity of nature rather than an affectation in the service of deception, as some malicious tongue-waggers would have it. What was charming beneath this coarse covering was that genuine expression that he gave to his invocations in his dealings with the possessed worshippers. Listening to him invoke his gods while singing strange songs; watching the tears fall from his glowing eyes; seeing him indicate with meaningful gestures sometimes the earth, sometimes the sky, smiling now and then through his tears, one asks oneself if this hieratic language truly does not conceal his poetry, but a naive, childlike poetry, fresh and full of grace like that of the peoples of antiquity. Each song elicits from your body a tremor of joy or sadness. For all the feelings expressed in these songs are reflected in the face of the priest. What a gentle and pleasing curiosity, what a feast for artists in search of novelties if one could rescue this poetry from all the changes that spoil it! What a triumph if the African muse lets itself seduce? But alas! We have no hint of the secret of our fathers' language, and those few who retain some scraps of it prove to be egoists, misers, or are reduced to talking gibberish without knowing the meaning....

The next day, Monday, Frè Ti Dor arrived at the head of his worshippers or *hounsi*, his red neckerchief worn around his neck in place of a tie. Each *hounsi* carried a small bundle of linen on the head. On a donkey could be seen a kind of metal bar and an iron shaft, three drums of different sizes having a cylindrical shape ending in a conical trunk, covered on their upper parts with cowhide attached with thongs and pegs. The metal bar, that is the *hougan*; the first or largest of the drums, that's the *houn*; the second or midsize, the *hounsi*; the third or smallest, the *hounla*....

The society stopped in front of the gate. They had to carry out a ceremony before entering the courtyard.... Then and there, the *hounguenicon*, in her purest tones, sang a song for the occasion: *Acoyo, na salué drapeau-là, nous rivé.... Acoyo,* etc.

At the same time, from the linen she took satin flags, spangled in the national colours, and presented them to two *hounsi* who came to gird up their loins. With a certain grace, they whirled to the right, to the left, sank to their knees, kissed the earth three times and took the flags held out to them. The *houguenicon* lifted them together and made them twirl. Laplace Ti Djo, having taken the machete from its sheath, placed himself in the centre of the flag carriers; and all three began their drills. The two women let the banners float, and one could see inscribed in sparkling letters the words 'Fleurs-de-Dahomey' – that was the name of the society.

Antoine Innocent
Mimola, 1906

The thief of the 'petit-bon-ange'

Novelist Jacques Stephen Alexis was also an untiring fighter for freedom. In an ironic twist, he was captured and killed at Môle-Saint-Nicolas, where Christopher Columbus landed. In this short extract from Les Arbres musiciens, *he evokes the atmosphere of mystery that surrounds the preparations for a ceremony.*

The offerings piled up before the altars of the *hounforts*; the dugouts loaded with wines, liqueurs, cakes, flowers and fruit were pushed out into the lake. Agouet Arroyo, the god of the waters, was the father of the area; it was necessary to assuage his hunger, quench his thirst, and send to him a vessel in which, eating their preferred foods and tipsy with the alcoholic spirits, the *Lwa* will approach the bank and make the sign their children are waiting for. What are the clouds saying? What are the winds singing? What are the *houngans* with their ever closed faces announcing? If the produce brings a good price, we will not want for our needs this year, that is certain, but is it all? A sure peace has never been known in this lake area. Always, at the moment when it is least expected, a landowner, a section chief or his aide, a lieutenant, or some other beast of prey will show up to claim something....

The *halefort* striking his loins, a knotted kerchief around his head, wearing an enormous straw hat, Danger Dossous, the *bocor* with an owlish eye, prowls around the village and with the end of his walking stick draws circles in the dust. He has been restless for several days already. He finally sets off toward the town. As he crosses the marketplace, silence follows his steps. Only some Dominican peasants, come to the marketplace to sell, whispered, pointing out to those who did not recognize him the *ganganmacoute,* implacable enemy of Bois-d'Orme Létiro, the majestic *papaloa,* patriarch and protector of the area. The mothers slapped the fingers of their imprudent children who dared to point to the impure man capable of taking from humans their *petit-bon-ange.* The earth had a mysterious resonance, the odour of inevitable events circulated in the air. The *donpèdre,* responding to the impalpable signs, set off, heading for a rendezvous with the menace that he senses coming. With his measured and tragic step, his gigantic stature drawn up to its full height, his huge chest thrust forward, Danger Dossous strode up and down the village.

Jacques Stephen Alexis
Les Arbres musicien, 1957

The carnival of history

With Hadriana dans tous mes rêves, René Depestre *won the Renaudot Prize in 1988. The carnival joyously telescopes the people of a village and those of human history.*

For the moment, musicians and dancers seemed to be camped out among their sleeping instruments: many kinds of drums, *vaccines, lambis,* rattles, saxophones, flutes, horns, accordions....

I stopped first before a group of men costumed as women. To simulate a state of advanced pregnancy, they placed pillows and cushions under their green satin dresses. They had the chests and buttocks of a callipygian Venus. Leaning against their clubs, the masqueraders chatted with characters draped in white sheets. These latter had their ears and nostrils stopped with cotton. They spoke in nasal tones. A few steps from these false dead huddled together several half-naked werewolves, glazed from head to foot with sugarcane syrup and lampblack. Their fingers ended in cone-shaped tin nails that clicked at the slightest movement. Between their teeth and their lips, they clenched pieces of orange peel, which gave their faces a frightful expression....

Near the music kiosk, I discovered a long line of Pierrots wearing motley-coloured clothes, pale blue gauze masks, and bells at their belts. In the area of the prefecture, some Carib Indians, with their brilliant feathers, gave their due to a demijohn of rum, their bows and arrows piled up on the sidewalk. The prefect's parrot, disguised as a

The celebration of carnival in Haiti reaches its high point during the three days before Ash Wednesday, in which all the shadowed, hidden or repressed aspects of society at every level can be freely expressed. Voodoo makes a strong showing in this feast of the imagination. Thus, some groups assume the costumes of devils, werewolves and zombies, conforming exactly to the traditional stories of Haitian voodoo.

vulture, repeated their bantering: 'To your health, you lousy Indians!'

The masqueraders had reconstituted on the square the time and the space that corresponded exactly to the heroes they represented, at the moment of their participation in history on the planet. But the historic memory had jumbled and blurred to the point of mockery, just like the tracks that led one after the other from the Capitoline to the Tarpeian rock....

The masquerade had called up three

centuries of human history....
The figures sculpted of the purest marble, like figurines of rotten wood, were together preparing to dance, to sing, to drink rum, to grouse at death, in raising the dust of the Place d'Armes of my village, which, in the middle of the universal masquerade, could be taken for the cosmic stage of the universe.

René Depestre
Hadriana dans tous mes rêves,
1988

The black star of hatred

Through the intervention of Ti-Jean Sandor, who seems to possess him, poet René Depestre here tries to exorcise hatred for the American invader, and more profoundly for the colonial slaveowner.

Ti-Jean Sandor
I am Ti-Jean Sandor
I am Prince Sandor
I am a cock with skinny feet
I am Ti-Jean with dry feet
I perch my heart
On the top of a palm tree
I use both hands
I walk backwards
Arms crossed in back
In front of me I explode
Charges of gunpowder
Behind me I leave
A long wake of chains
I change my West-Point cadet
Into a beautiful pedigree dog
Whose ear I bite
I am a great eater
Of white dogs I am
A bull with one hundred balls
I change my Yale student
Into a boiler with three legs
I am bakoulou-baka . . .
The hate never leaves my bones

Nor my blood nor my skin
Even when I sleep at night
Its black star opens eyes in me
That are claws
If I am left to go to the limit
Of my night of gall I will bind
My muscles to those of cyclone
And earthquake
To engulf this bitter South
And the other South furrowed
In the side of my Africa
O Hate my great health
I plunge my burning temples
In the icy blue of your waves
I plunge my people naked
In this proud purifying current
I plunge our tigers our spears
Our wounds our cries our thirsts
Our feathers our knives our tears
Into this whirlwind of holy water
And here we are
All the black convicts of this world
Baptized forever
Here we are finally ripe enough
To give to our conspiracies

Great white wings
Like the orgies of hate
In the white heart of the South!

René Depestre
*A Rainbow for
the Christian West*, trans. Joan Dayan,
1977

Baron-la-Croix and the dictator

The exchanges between the 'Chief' and General Baron-la-Croix in Franck Fouché's play clearly make allusion to the bloody events on Haiti's 'stage' under the Duvalier dictatorship.

(The lighting will naturally add to the creation of a climate of delirium and mass hysteria. Dressed for the occasion, the Chief wears the regalia of an officer, *asson* and sword in his hands. He cross-examines Baron-la-Croix after having traced on the ground *vèvè* symbolic of the spirit or *lwa*.)

CHIEF: Tell me, general, what do you do to hold power for 2000 years?

BARON-LA-CROIX (laughs): 2000 years! But, great chief, that's almost an eternity you're asking for. You seem very demanding.

CHIEF: No, not really. I am simply aware of my historic mission. It's just that life is short in the face of what I, chief, promise for my people.

B.-LA-C.: This belongs to the realm of the great Beelzebub, prince of Hell. As for me, my powers are less brilliant. (He laughs)

CHIEF: Me, I'm ready for whatever the great Beelzebub asks. If this is the price of my lasting…holding power forever.

B.-LA-C. (laughs): I warn you, the gods

A performance of *Général Baron-la-Croix* at Avignon.

François Duvalier Receiving the 'Oungan' on his Deathbed, a painting by Gérard Valcin.

of Hell want cadavers, always cadavers. You cannot imagine their thirst, their ravenous hunger for cadavers. You understand, at our century's end, there's not another good war of extermination or, as in the old days, a nice epidemic of plague or cholera. You see, with the progress science has made today, people no longer dying, the planet becoming full like an egg, what an overpeopling that can create. No space for anyone, no food for anyone. With all the raw weight of fat, of hair, of excrement, the equilibrium is broken for good. There won't be anything left for the planet but to explode or jump into the abyss. Therefore … (little cat laugh) it is necessary that death rule, rule without end, to make way for life! (He breaks out in a macabre laugh)

CHIEF: I tell you, general, I'm ready, ready for anything. Let the gods command!

B.-LA-C.: Among other things, they also need living sacrifices for the marriage of spirit with matter. (Short pause) In this transaction with the princes of Hell, I, Baron-la-Croix, can serve as your intermediary: for example, present your offerings as matters for study. They are material evidence that will allow them to see if you have the substance and the heart of a man aspiring to glory and immortality.

Franck Fouché
Général Baron-la-Croix
1970

Dance, music and songs

Catherine Dunham was one of the first to have tried and succeeded at using voodoo dances in a modern context. To that end, she researched the profound and universal significance of the sacred gestures. Likewise, the various rhythms of voodoo music, popularized since the

Boukman Expérians.

The logo of the musical group Ram integrates images from voodoo mythology.

Catherine Dunham at the Théâtre de Paris in 1948.

1950s by Martha Jean-Claude and Emérante de Pradines, today have been restored to a place of honour and have reappeared, enriched by contact with American pop, in such internationally known groups as Boukman Expérians and Ram. Many of these groups, called groupes-racines *(root-groups)*, have stirred young people with their recognition of the positive cultural values of voodoo.

Songs from the worship of voodoo have been generously used in most musical creations in Haiti, for which they serve as a continuous source of inspiration. Each lwa *corresponds to its own rhythm of the drum, as well as its song, which is given voice at the moment when he enters the body of one of his servants.*

Danbala Wèdo se bon se bon
Ayida Wèdo se bon se bon
Lè ma moute chwal mwen
Gen moun ka kriye
Lè ma moute chwal mwen
Gen san ka vèse
Lè ma moute chwal mwen
Gen moun ka kriye

Vèvè of Taureau, Simbi, Grand Bois and so on.

The Creole text can be translated:
Dambala Wèdo we shall see
Ayida Wèdo we shall see
When in my turn I will be in a trance
I see already who will spill tears
When in my turn I will be possessed
I see already who will pay with their blood

Presented by Claude Dauphin in *Musique du Vaudou*, 1986

more influence on Haitian painting. The *vèvè* have also been the subject of studies and research for numerous Haitian artists, 'naive' or 'sophisticated', who, aware of their decorative value, have thought to integrate them into their works.... When one realizes the wealth of this repertory, one cannot but be astonished at the adroitness of the 'makers' of *vèvè*, which predisposes them already to other graphic

Hector Hyppolite, *Loa-Boa*.

Voodoo and Haitian painting

In December 1975, critic André Malraux discovered the community of painters in Saint-Soleil, in which he saw 'the most thrilling experience – and the only one that can be verified – of magical painting in our century'. Michel Philippe Lerebours, author of the book Haiti and its painters, from 1804 to 1980, *ascertains the undeniable dynamism that the invisible world of voodoo gives to Haitian artists.*

The importance of Christian chromolithographs in the choice of tonalities and the placement of colour harmonies cannot be denied, but the *vèvè*, one of the elements essential to the voodoo religion, seems to have

works. Let us not forget that many Haitian artists – Hector Hyppolite, André Pierre, Lafortune Félix – before becoming painters started out as 'makers' of *vèvè*.

Primitive Haitian painting draws its power by equalling the reality of Haitian life, which itself cannot be understood without reference to voodoo. Certainly, it is not always necessary to know voodoo in order to understand and interpret a Haitian painting. For example, when Hector Hyppolite represents *Le Dieu tout puissant* [The almighty God, p. 64] with his three eyes, that could strike us as strange or naive. In reality, he has painted not the Christian God but the Great Master of voodoo theology: 'Great Master nine toes', one might repeat, all the while taking care to specify that he has five toes on each foot.

In the voodoo liturgy, each colour has a particular meaning, and painting submits to its influence, whether the painter realizes it or not.… Lines also have a cosmic value. The vertical represents the spirit; the horizontal, matter; the cross becomes the meeting of spirit and matter, the sign of Legba, who provides access to the other *lwa;* it is also the sign of Christ, god becoming man. The circle, which appears one way or another in almost all the *vèvè*, is not only the symbol of Dambala, the snake *lwa,* but is also the image of humans who become the centre of everything.

Michel Philippe Lerebours
in *Haïti: art naïf, art vaudou*
1988

The flow of the essential

The author of Années Dessaline, la famille Vortex *and* Jacmel au crépuscule, *among other books, Jean Metellus gives this moving testimonial in* Haiti, une nation pathétique.

Voodoo as it is experienced by Haitian painters does not belong to the past. And if Galilee has not definitively thinned the blood of Catholicism, it would need events otherwise more important than electricity and tractors in Haitian campaigns to exorcise voodoo completely.

Haitian painting tries to restore the confused thread of the birth and the history of the Haitian people; it redraws on the torn cloth of its customs all of its original resources, its opening up and possibilities of access to the world; it is the flow of the essential, of vegetation, of grace in the expression of the world. It is our capacity for richness that is seized. This great mystic flux, this warm human circulation, this indecipherable divine expansion, this bewitching presence of the *lwa* in Valcin's painting *Scène de vaudou* [Voodoo scene], in short, the whole of the painting forbids us to make reference to any context other than Haiti.

Jean Metellus
Haïti, une nation pathétique, 1987

With the film *White Zombie* (1932) came the birth of cinematic voodoo, a subject that soon burgeoned in the genre of Hollywood horror films. Since that time voodoo has been represented in the cinema – and thus, exists in the Western imagination – as a satanic cult threatening to upset the status quo with zombies, black magic, sorcery and human sacrifice. This imagery has served to reinforce racist attitudes and negative stereotypes of black culture. Madeleine, opposite, is the white zombie that brought shivers of fear to cinemagoers.

People travel, so do spirits

Among those who practise voodoo around the world today, three major 'families' stand out: the original religion, which began and remains in Africa; voodoo imported into the Americas with the slaves; and a more recent form, tied to the mostly Haitian diaspora as voodoo followers emigrate and settle in more industrialized countries.

M anifestation of Yémanja, queen of the waters, in Bahian *candomblé*.

Almost everywhere in the Americas where communities of black people have settled the worship of voodoo has retained its vitality – for example, in South America, in such countries as Brazil, Colombia, Ecuador and Venezuela. It is also widespread throughout the Caribbean, sometimes in attenuated form, sometimes equivalent to Haitian voodoo, like the Cuban form called santería. *By contrast, in the Dominican Republic, voodoo is considered a purely Haitian religion, comparable to magic and sorcery. In reality, the* lwa *are still honoured there, within the framework of pious church brotherhoods or societies and tied to the liturgical calendar.*

Brazil: all the saints from Bahia

Under the name of candomblé, *African religions have thrived in Brazil.*

Oldest and purest of the tribal cults in Brazil is *candomblé*. It is practised most frequently in Bahia, though its influence is beginning to spread as far south as São Paulo. Only in *candomblé* are the ties with Africa nurtured – and even renewed through visits and the importation of cult objects like raffia and cowry shells. *Candomblé* is a conservative religion. Not only do *candomblé*'s devotees place great stress on the *orixás*' African names and identities, preserving the Nagô-Yoruba words in their incantations, but they also tend to be group-oriented and not political. They rarely if ever go into trance spontaneously, and they place the cult's major emphases on ritual and divination, initiation and sacrifice.

Who are the deities of *candomblé*? How are they worshipped? And for what reasons?

Corresponding to Christianity's all-powerful 'God' is *Olorún,* significantly not worshipped at all either in West Africa or in Brazil because he is considered too mighty to be concerned with the trials and trivia of mere mortals. *Oxalá* is the most exalted member of the Yoruba pantheon. Son of *Olorún,* he is father of the other gods, sovereign healer, spirit of pro-creation, bi-sexual. Other important deities in *candomblé* are *Iemanjá* (Our Lady of Conception), the sea-goddess now represented as a mermaid; *Omolú* (Saint Lazarus), fearsome master of plagues, diseases and death, who may not be looked in the face and who therefore 'appears' at rites masked; *Xangô* (Saint Jerome), Thor-like god of thunder and fire, especially popular in Rio de Janiero and Recife; *Iansa* (Saint Barbara), *Xangô*'s wife, who dances aggressively, brandishing a copper scimitar; *Oxossi,* the hunter who carries a bow; *Ogoun,* divine blacksmith, god of war, patron of handicrafts and industry; and *Exú,* incorrectly identified with the devil but derived from the West African *Legba,* messenger of the gods. *Exú,* a trickster who must be placated before the other gods are invoked, haunts the crossroads; he is venal, facetious, phallic, violent, not to be trifled with.

As in Haitian *vaudun* (and all other cults derived from West Africa), 'possession' is central, for unless the devotee or his intercessor among the *filhas* (handmaidens) of the *máe de santo* (high priestess) loses earthly identity during the ceremony and becomes the deity invoked, no communication with the higher world is possible, and none of the worshipper's problems will be solved.

Partly because Bahian (and African

tribal) society is matriarchal, and partly because males have less time to concentrate and are more accessible to influences outside the African-Brazilian community, the officials of the cult are almost invariably female, and very few males are susceptible to possession. The *máe de santo* may be a *feiticero* (dealer in black magic), but in most *terreiros* (temples) putting harmful spells on one's enemies is not countenanced. Sacrificing doves and goats at appropriate rites, leading prayers and dances, are among her functions. The *máe* is always a specialist in the use of herbs to cure minor ailments, and she is adept at foretelling a believer's future by 'reading the shells' (*búzios*). She and her *filhas* regularly attend Mass, and sometimes all of the *candomblé* personnel participate in Catholic church functions – much to the delight of the Bahian Roman hierarchy, which exercises great tact, believing that their faith will win the ultimate allegiance.

One day in Salvador we were lucky enough to attend two *candomblé* rites. The first, very informal, was a baptismal get-together at the waterfalls outside the city known as Cachoeira de São Bartolomeo. Hundreds of Bahians of both sexes and all ages crowded around the steep cascade, whose rock face was decorated with votive candles and little piles of farina-like cotton balls. A battery of three drums, interspersed with chants in the Yoruba tongue, summoned the *orixás.* Many of those who let the falling waters hit them were instantly possessed, shaking spasmodically. We noticed one dressed in the uniform of an Esso gas station attendant. Children, unconcerned, splashed joyously in the lower pools. Market women sold food and soft drinks. A homemade cross bore the three words AMOR, DEUS, PAZ.

A more formal ceremony took place at night at the *terreiro* of *Axé Opô Afonjá,* a very large one open at the sides behind the spectators' benches. Pennants of red and white paper hung from the thatched roof over the earthen floor. On an elevated platform at the far end, the ample, impassive *máe* in her billowing white robes was enthroned amid her court, from time to time shaking her symbol of authority, the conelike silver bell. As we came in, the drumming had already started, and the dozen or more *filhas* in their hooped skirts and sequined blouses were dancing barefooted in an ellipse, gesturing with their hands.

First the *Exú* received his conciliatory chant, in which he was implored not to make his unwanted presence manifest. Next the *filhas* made bow-and-arrow gestures for *Oxossi,* the hunter. And then, as the drum rhythms shifted subtly, they began to abase themselves before the *máe,* from a prone position first kissing one foot and then the other. The rhythms shifted abruptly now to greet *Iansa,* goddess of storms and thunder. Many of the *filhas* went into trance, some making plaintive animal cries and rocking around the enclosure as if desperate to escape. *Oxumaré,* the serpent god, was called. But the *filhas* were now drifting out to remain entranced until their re-entry as *santos.* *Omolú's* music was played. Cat-cries followed, and a spectator in one corner began to thrash about convulsively. Chants of 'Agolana!' Intermission.

The *filhas,* now dressed for their new role as saints, began to come back, all but one representing females. That one, *Omolú,* was gorgeously arrayed in strands of raffia, which fell from her helmet of cowry shells to cover her face and body. Others wore heavy arm-bangles, face-screens of copper beads. Some brandished battle-axes, poniards, powder-horns, mirrors, bundles of sticks. One of the masked ones left the dance to kiss us on both cheeks – exactly as in Haitian *vaudun*! The ceremony would continue till dawn.

Selden Rodman and Carole Cleaver
Spirits of the Night: The Vaudun Gods
of Haiti,
1992

Voodoo in the Haitian diaspora

In 1992, an estimated one million Haitians left their country for others (Dominican Republic, the United States,

A young initiate in Brooklyn.

Canada, French departments in the Caribbean, France). Despite the problems of re-creating a receptive environment in which voodoo can thrive, the lwa *continue to receive the honours due them, tightening the bonds of their servants with their native soil.*

The lwa *do not travel at the same time as the émigré, but itinerant* oungan *and* manbo *carry them in the form of sachets and packets, necklaces, or bottles filled with ingredients for the protective baths. Oufò are established, perhaps in the basements of apartment houses, notably in Brooklyn, New York, or the Parisian suburbs.*

Voodoo in Brooklyn

Karen McCarthy Brown, an American anthropologist, presents the spiritual biography of a manbo *and her family in* Mama Lola: A Vodou Priestess in Brooklyn. *In it, she traces the road followed by Alourdes, subjected to various misfortunes, until her initiation after she receives messages from the* lwa *Dambala in her dreams.*

Bad luck, the broadest diagnostic category in the lexicon of the Vodou healing system, can be a one-time thing such as a car accident, a lost job, or an illness; or it can be a shift in the quality of life that affects everything – which was how Alourdes and Maggie diagnosed their situation in early 1981.

Everything went wrong, small things (lost keys, jammed doors, mail that did not arrive) and big ones. The trouble started when the heating pipes froze and burst in January. Less than two weeks later, Maggie lost her job and contracted chicken pox. The bad luck then began to spread, as it is known to do, to vulnerable others (those not

spiritually protected) who were connected to them. Gabriel, Alourdes's former boyfriend, who was living with them at the time, was mugged. Alourdes's son William was arrested for purse snatching.

When bad luck is pervasive, 'you got to pay attention to that', as Alourdes put it. But in order to pay attention, a person has to be centered and calm enough to sleep well, dream frequently, and remember those dreams. By early March, the anxiety level in the house had risen so high that when the spirits sent Maggie a dream warning her about the next link in the chain of bad luck, she did not remember it right away, and, when she did remember, she misinterpreted a key element:

They warn me. They tell me about that. I just have too many thing in my head. I forget about it. I just been running around trying to do too many thing. But I dream.... I dream that I come home one night and find my door open, and I go in there and look, and there are four horses looking at me right from the fire escape. They just standing there looking at me, and then I hear something in the front of my apartment, you know, in the bedroom, and I go in there…and there is Joe. You know Joe? Aileen's son. And I say to him, 'What you doing in here? What you doing in my apartment?' And he tell me he just come in looking for something. And I get real mad and just sock him, beat him up! And throw him out!

In mid-March, a few days after this dream, the row house in Fort Greene was robbed, the first burglary they had experienced in nearly twenty years of living there. Maggie occupies the second-floor apartment, below the one rented out to Aileen and her son, Joe. The burglar got onto the fire escape in back and came in through Maggie's kitchen window, where the horses were standing in her dream. Maggie lost the engagement ring that Raphael Sanchez, Michael's father, had given her; a jar full of quarters; a collection of foreign money; and a new camera for which she had yet to make her first payment.… Maggie had not realized how directly the spirits were speaking to her.

The robbery clinched Maggie's diagnosis about the cause of the period of bad luck. She decided it was definitely a result of harassment by the spirits, who were demanding that she stop postponing her initiation. It had been almost two years since the important dream in which she had sworn to Danbala that she would return to Haiti to take the *ason*. Work and financial troubles, she said, had prevented her from fulfilling her promises right away.… In fact, during the two years since her promise to Papa Danbala, Maggie had been struggling mightily with the consequences of taking on the responsibilities of a *manbo*.
Karen McCarthy Brown
Mama Lola: A Vodou Priestess in Brooklyn,
1991

'The Mysteries understand that we are far from home': voodoo in Paris

When they get the opportunity, they work as waiters, cabdrivers, housekeepers, cooks, musicians, seamstresses, bookkeepers or secretaries. In Paris, Haitians 'look for life' with shrewdness and courage. In this setting of life on the edge, where luck,
jealousy and rivalry dominate daily events, voodoo serves as a weapon in the struggle against despair and solitude.
Oungan *and* manbo *receive followers in the housing projects in the 20th arrondissement, the slums of Barbès. Many hold their services in the suburbs – Villejuif, Monfermeil, Aubervilliers. The author of* Racines du vodou *and a novel titled* Les Chemins de Loco Miroir, *Lilas Desquiron learned from one of these priestesses the problems of practising in a cultural context far different from one's original culture.*

They carry on a pitiless struggle for clients. They rarely meet but happily get hold of malicious gossip about each other. Parisians from the Antilles, Martinique and Guadeloupe mix freely with the faithful from Haiti, which explains the inter-Caribbean Creole heard in Parisian *oufò*. Their greatest problems: the impossility of beating the sacred drums at night and the lack of earthen floors to drink the blood of sacrifices and to transmit the power of ancestors to bare feet.

Madame Guédélia, who practises at Stains, recently arrived with her Guadeloupian husband: 'I was working in a restaurant in Guadeloupe when I met him and he brought me here. I had not yet been initiated, but when I learned I had to go as far away as France, I returned to "my country", in the south of Haiti, near Les Cayes, to make ceremonies, greet the *lwa*, feed them so they would open the gate to me. That was in 1973. In 1980 I went to Haiti to give a *manjé-lwa* and make them my promise. In 1986 I was initiated, and I took up the heritage of my mother, who served 101 *lwa-Guinen*.'

Madame Guédélia lived in the

shadow of the cathedral of France's kings. In the stone houses surrounding it, she had her faithful: 'Here in France, I advertised, I sent out my cards and people came to me. Many from Martinique, Guadeloupe, Guyana, white France, too. I get very few Haitians. They come, but not many. I give them the "luck baths" so they can find work, love, I undo spells if they have too much bad luck, or I give them a consultation on their future. I also prepare perfumes that act as powerful charms.'

Haitian friends, mixing with the regular clientele, come for the *'service kay'*, the big annual ceremony in honour of the house *lwa;* but even here, exile transforms everything: 'Everything in my temple, my stones, the *assein* of Ogoun, my Baron cross, the *po-tèt*, all these things I brought from Haiti after my initiation. The ground, it's a bit of Haitian earth I had to mix with earth from here to make the small mound where I placed my stone. You can imagine how heavy my suitcases were for that trip! I don't have a *poteau-mitan*. There are things I just can't do. For example, the fire bath of Ogoun: I set fire to the carpet! As to leaves that can't be found here, each time I go back to my country, I dry them; they are there when I need them.'

Does voodoo in exile run the risk of losing its soul? 'The Mysteries understand that we are far from home', Madame Guédélia replies gently.

Lilas Desquiron

Yesterday, today, family or royal: the 'vodun' of ancient Dahomey

On 29 April 1962, a delegation of legislators of Dahomey, led by the president of the National Assembly and the president of the Supreme Court, met at Allada with 1832 priests from lower and middle Dahomey to discuss common problems at every level. What could justify on the part of the authorities such 'consideration, composed of fear, questioning and admiration'? Honorat Aguessy sought the justification in the past.

In ancient Dahomey, in what is now known as the Gulf of Guinea, the existence of *vodun* at the level of the family, kinship and region was a living reality. Its existence at every social level was equally strong. This explains the great number of 'convents' or places of worship today.

Like every other family, the royal family had its vodun.

Each kinship line has its own exteriorization or nomination of *vodun* called *toxwio* – founding ancestor – to which is added Ayizan. *Toxwio* represents, in a sense, the indispensable condition for the institutional recognition of a lineage.… It represents the memory of the eponymous ancestor, that is, the first recognized and knowable ancestor in the lineage.…

V oodoo festival in Ouidah, 1992, at the royal palace of Porto-Novo.

Besides the *vodun* tied to the different kinship lines, there are *vodun* common to all of society…considered at its furthest imaginable limits or boundaries. This is where a multitude of *vodun* emerges, categorized in the pantheon of the sky, in the pantheon of the earth, or in the pantheon of water, and whose functions cover all the physical, social and moral realms concerning the life of the society.… These common or public *vodun*, identified next to the family *vodun*, give an idea of the richness in the religious domain, for they not only register the preoccupations and aspirations common to the entire society, they also reveal how the individual, bearing in mind his fate and his shortcomings or wants, can fulfil the familial religious archetype. In this sense, the individual, through the subterfuge of Fa and bearing in mind his personal radiance, can cleave to a *vodun* that allows him to feel he has found the solution to his shortcomings or wants. Thus to the family *vodun* are added the public *vodun* (local and national).

Where did these public *vodun* come from? From gradual acquisition, alliance, purchase and war. Every king tried to take back from his expeditions the *vodun* he met where the war was carried on. He brought them back, along with their priest and his entire group. It is remarkable that among the prized spoils the kings of Dahomey coveted was the acquisition of *vodun*. Thus war facilitated the diffusion and mixture of cults. Most of the *vodun* bought from neighbours were on the suggestion or command of Fa. This was the case of Sakpata, introduced in Agbomê to check the plague of smallpox that had decimated the royal army in the war against the Honji.

The king undertook to bring together and organize these different acquired *vodun*, especially at Abomey, the royal capital … assigning them complementary functions. The *vodun* of the royal capital were more numerous than those of the provinces, as if the political capital, which was also the main religious seat, had the awareness to insure to it alone all the protection and security of not only the palace but also of the entire country.

Honorat Aguessy
'Réligion africaine et rapport des forces',
UNESCO, 24–28 June 1985

Haitian voodoo practised in Brooklyn (above and opposite).

GLOSSARY

Asòtò: drum.
Asson: rattle of the voodoo priest or priestess, symbol of spiritual power.
Bòkò: a voodoo priest who uses sorcery.
Dansé-lwa: the 'fit of possession' in a voodoo ritual.
Dessounen: rite that separates the 'spirit' attached to an initiate, just before or after his or her death.
Gédé: 'spirits' of the dead.
Govi: pitcher containing the 'spirits'.
Gwo-bon anj: one of two spiritual principles of the individual, with *ti-bon anj*.
Lwa: 'spirit' of the voodoo religion.
Lwa-achté: spirit purchased as insurance against misfortune.
Lwa-mèt-tèt: protective 'spirit' received at the time of initiation.
Lwa-rasin: 'spirit' inherited through the family.

Manbo: voodoo priestess.
Manjé-lwa: sacrifice in a voodoo ritual.
Oufò: voodoo temple.
Oungan: voodoo priest.
Ounsi: voodoo initiate.
Peristyle: open shed in the voodoo temple where the ritual dances take place.
Po-tèt: pot containing hair and nail clippings of a dead initiate.
Poteau-mitan: post in the centre of the peristyle that is the means by which the *lwa* arrive among humans.
Pwen: 'supernatural' power or magical protective force.
Ti-bon anj: one of two spiritual principles of the individual, with *gwo-bon anj*.
Vèvè: symbolic drawing of the *lwa*.
Wanga: evil charm.

CHRONOLOGY

1492 Christopher Columbus lands in Haiti at Môle-Saint-Nicolas.
1503 Introduction of the first black slaves to the island, called Hispaniola by the conquistadores.
1635 The Compagnie des Iles de l'Amérique is created to carry on the slave trade of black people.
1664 The Compagnie des Indes Occidentales is created for the French possessions of the Antilles. France names Bertrand d'Ogeron governor of Saint-Domingue, the name given by the French to the part of Hispaniola that they had settled.
1685 Promulgation of the Black Code.
1697 Treaty of Ryswick signed in which Spain cedes to France a third of the island of Hispaniola.
1750–8 The Maroon François Makandal carries on a campaign of terror through poisoning among the white colonials.
1791 Voodoo ceremony of Bois-Caïman is held, preparatory to the general slave insurrection of 22 August.
1793 L. F. Sonthonax, member of a civil commission sent by the French National Convention, announces the emancipation of the slaves.
1797 Abbé Grégoire sends priests belonging to the civil constitution of the clergy to Toussaint-Louverture, governor of Saint-Domingue.
1802 Napoleon sends troops under the direction of General Leclerc to reestablish slavery on Saint-Domingue. In ensuing battles, the French fight against black and mulatto generals Jean-Jacques Dessalines, Alexandre Pétion and Henri Christophe.

1804 Haiti is proclaimed independent; Dessalines made governor for life.
1806 Dessalines assassinated.
1818–43 Rule by president Jean-Pierre Boyer who establishes Haiti's rural code (1826) and penal code (1835), mandating fines and punishments for the practice of voodoo.
1844 Santo Domingo (now the Dominican Republic) is founded in the Spanish portion of the island.
1860 Concordat between the Haitian government and the Vatican is signed, followed by first 'antisuperstitious' campaign in 1864.
1896 With the support of the government, the Church leads an 'antisuperstitious' campaign in every parish in the country; subsequent campaigns in 1912, 1925–30, 1940–1.
1915–34 Occupation of Haiti by US Marines.
1957–86 Dictatorship of the Duvaliers (father and son).
1987 A new constitution is approved. The Creole language is recognized as an official language of the country, along with French. Voodoo is decriminalized.
16 December 1990 The Reverend Jean-Bertrand Aristide is elected president of Haiti with sixty-seven per cent of the vote in an election supervised by United Nations observers.
29 September 1991 The army stages a violent coup d'état; the elected president goes into exile.
15 October 1994 After three years of military rule, Aristide is reinstated as the legitimate president of Haiti.

FURTHER READING

Alexis, Jacques Stephen, *Les Arbres Musiciens*, 1957

Brown, Karen McCarthy, *Mama Lola: A Vodou Priestess in Brooklyn*, 1991

Courlander, H., *The Drum and the Hoe, Life and Lore of Haïtian People*, 1960; and Richard P. Schaedel, *Religion and Politics in Haiti*, 1966

Dauphin, Claude, *Musique du Vaudou*, 1986

Davis, Wade, *The Serpent and the Rainbow*, 1986

Debien, G., *Les Esclaves aux Antilles Françaises (XVIIe–XVIIIe Siècle)*, 1974

Depestre, René, *A Rainbow for the Christian West*, trans. Joan Dayan, 1977; *Hadriana dans tous mes rêves*, 1988

Deren, Maya, *Divine Horsemen: The Voodoo Gods*, 1953

Desmangles, Leslie G., *The Faces of the Gods: Vodou and Roman Catholicism in Haiti*, 1992

Dunham, Catherine, *Island Possessed*, 1969

Fick, Carolyn E., *The Making of Haiti: The Saint Domingue Revolution from Below*, 1990

Gilfond, Harry, *Voodoo, its Origins and Practices*, 1976

Herskovits, Melville J., *Life in a Haitian Valley*, 1937

Hurbon, Laënnec, *Dieu dans le Vaudou Haïtien*, 1987; *Culture et dictature en Haïti, l'imaginaire sous contrôle*; *Le Barbare imaginaire*, 1988; *Comprendre Haïti: Essai sur l'Etat, la Nation, la Culture*, 1987

Hurston, Zora Neale, *Tell My Horse*, 1938

Labat, Jean-Baptiste, *The Memoirs of Pere Labat, 1693–1705*, trans. John Eaden, 1931

Laguerre, M. S., *Voodoo and Politics in Haïti*, 1989

Lerebours, Michel Philippe, *Haïti: Art Naïf, Art Vaudou*, exhibition catalogue, 1988

Madiou, Th., *Histoire d'Haïti*, 8 vols., 1989

Metellus, *Haïti, une nation pathétique*, 1987

Métraux, Alfred, *Voodoo in Haiti*, trans. Hugo Charteris, 1972

Moreau de Saint-Méry, L. E., *Description topographique, physique, civile, politique et historique de la partie française de l'ile de Saint-Domingue*, 2 vols., 1797

Murphy, Joseph, *Working the Spirit: Ceremonies of the African Diaspora*, 1994

Pelton, Robert Wayne, *Voodoo Signs and Omens*, 1986

Peters, Carl Edward, *La Croix contre l'asson*, 1960

Price-Mars, Jean, *So Spoke the Uncle*, trans. Magdaline W. Shannon, 1983

Rodman, Selden, and Carole Cleaver, *Spirits of the Night: The Vaudun Gods of Haiti*, 1992

Roumain, J., *A propos de la campagne antisuperstitieuse*, 1942; *Masters of the Dew* (1947), trans. Langston Hughes and Mercer Cook, 1972

Tomorrow (Quarterly), special Haiti issue (vol. 3, no. 4), Autumn 1954

Trouillot, Michel-Rolph, *Haiti, State Against Nation: The Origins and Legacy of Duvalierism*, 1990

Williams, Sheldon, *Voodoo and the Art of Haiti*, 1969

LIST OF ILLUSTRATIONS

The following abbreviations have been used:
a above; *b* below; *c* centre; *l* left; *r* right;
BN Bibliothèque Nationale, Paris; MH Musée de l'Homme, Paris

COVER

Front Edouard Duval Carrie, *Le Couple Infernal – Baron Samedi et Marinette Bois Chêche*, left panel of diptych, 1991. Collection of the artist
Spine Statue of Dos Diable
Back Voodoo ceremony at Nan Soukri

OPENING

CHAPTER 1

CHAPTER 2

INDEX

ACKNOWLEDGMENTS

The author and the publishers wish to thank Afrique en création, Henri-Robert Deschamps, Lilas Desquiron, Bernard Diederich, Didier Dominique, Jean Marie Drot and Michel Ménard P.S.J. (Pères de la Compagnie Saint-Jacques), whose work and advice greatly contributed towards the realization of this book.

PHOTO CREDITS

Afrique en création/Aldo Vacchina, Paris 22, 26–7, 32, 40, 44–5, 46–7, 55a, 57, 69, 74a, 86–7, 114–5, 119r, 123. Agence Bernand 156b. Agence Bernand/Sanvi Panou 154. Agence France Presse, Paris 118b. Agence Métisse/Marie-Paule Nègre 165. All rights reserved 46b, 129, 140, 143, 156a, 157a, 157b. Archives Gallimard 83b, 109b, 134. © Archives Gallimard/Alfred Métraux 63. © Archives Gallimard/Pierre Verger 110, 111al, 111ar. Archives Nationales, Paris 49a. Rachel Beauvoir-Dominique 66–7, 100. Bettman Archives, New York 54–5, 55b, 60–1. Bibliothèque Nationale, Paris 13, 14, 18–9, 19, 22, 23, 24a, 24b, 25a, 29, 31, 33, 34a, 34b, 34–5, 36a, 36b, 38, 38–9, 39, 41a, 46a, 48–9, 133, 169. British Film Institute, London 58a, 58b, 159. Cahiers du Cinéma, Paris 59. Centre Culturel Vincent Placoly, Marin, Martinique 1, 2, 3, 4, 5, 6, 7, 8, 9. Centre Georges Pompidou, Paris/K. Ignatiadis 144, 148a, 148b, 149. Charmet, Paris 18al, 51, 52. Dagli Orti, Paris 12, 20a, 20b, 21, 49al. Editions Henri Deschamps, Port-au-Prince, Haiti 37. Bernard Diederich, Palm Beach, Florida 62a, 62b, 64, 73, 112a, 112b, 118b, 122–3, 128, 153. Edouard Duval Carrie front cover. Edimédia spine. © Editions A.-M. Métaillé/Pierre Verger 160. Explorer/Chantal Regnault, Paris 68a, 70a, 74–5, 75, 76, 77al, 77ar, 77b, 78, 79, 81b, 82, 84, 85, 88b, 93a, 93b, 94, 95, 96, 97, 98, 99, 102a, 103, 104, 105, 106, 107b, 109a, 116, 117, 121a, 121c, 121b, 127, 147, 162, 166, 167a, 167b. Gamma, Paris 125. Michel Gardère, Haiti 70b, 86–7. Giraudon, Paris 42a. Grand Séminaire Saint-Jacques, Guiclan, Landivisiau 136–7. B. Hatala 145. Laënnec Hurbon, Port-au-Prince 81a. Nicolas Jallot, Paris 42, 48, 60bl, 61, 68b, 71b, 90, 102b, 124. Catherine Millet, Paris back cover, 107a, 126, 126–7, 155b. Musée Albert Khan, Paris 14–5, 17. Photothèque of the Musée de l'Homme, Paris 16l, 16ar, 16br. Photothèque of the Musée de l'Homme, Paris/J. Oster 150. Musée National d'Art Moderne, Centre Georges Pompidou, Paris 41b, 67, 80b. G. Namur/Lalance, Paris 25b, 42–3. Bernard Nantet, Paris 15a, 72a, 72c. Jean-Claude Pattacini, Paris 11, 88a, 89, 91, 92, 101a, 101b, 108a, 108b, 114, 118–9, 120. The Research Libraries, New York Public Library, New York 50, 56a, 56r, 56l. Roger Viollet, Paris 28, 30, 53.

TEXT CREDITS

Grateful acknowledgment is made for use of material from the following: (pp. 163–4) Karen Brown, *Mama Lola: A Vodou Priestess in Brooklyn*, University of California Press, 1991; copyright © 1991 The Regents of the University of California. (pp. 153–4) Reprinted from René Depestre, *A Rainbow for the Christian West*, trans. by Joan Dayan (Amherst: The University of Massachusetts Press, 1977); copyright © 1977 by Joan Dayan. (pp. 138–9) Reprinted from Leslie G. Desmangles, *The Faces of the Gods: Vodou and Roman Catholicism in Haiti;* copyright © 1992 by The University of North Carolina Press; used by permission of the publisher. (pp. frontispiece, 63, 88, 136–7) Excerpts from Alfred Métraux, *Voodoo in Haiti*, trans. Hugo Charteris, Schocken Books, New York, copyright © 1959 by Alfred Métraux; reprinted by permission of Schocken/Pantheon Books and Société Nouvelle Presence Africaine. (pp. 144–5) Excerpt from Jean Price-Mars, *So Spoke the Uncle*, as translated by Magdaline W. Shannon and as published by Three Continents Press; © M. W. Shannon, 1983. (pp. 160–2) Selden Rodman and Carole Cleaver, *Spirits of the Night: The Vaudun Gods of Haiti*, Spring Publications, 1992; © 1992 by Spring Publications, Inc. All rights reserved.

Laënnec Hurbon
is director of research at CNRS and
professor at the Quisqueya University in Port-au-
Prince, of which he is one of the founding members.
He has written many books on Haitian voodoo
and today focuses on the relationships
between religion, culture and politics.
Among his most recent publications are:
Le Barbare imaginaire (1988), *Comprendre Haïti*
(1987) and, under his direction,
Le Phénomène religieux dans la Caraïbe (1989).

© Gallimard 1993

English translation © Thames and Hudson Ltd,
London, 1995

Translated by Lory Frankel

British Library Cataloguing-in-Publication Data

A catalogue record for this book is available from
the British Library

ISBN 0–500–30049–6

Printed and bound in Italy
by Editoriale Libraria, Trieste